# Desert Cats

# Desert Cats

## The RAF's Jaguar Force in the First Gulf War

Danny Burt

**DESERT CATS**
**The RAF's Jaguar Force in the First Gulf War**

First published in Great Britain in 2023 by
Air World
An imprint of
Pen & Sword Books Ltd
Yorkshire – Philadelphia

Copyright © Danny Burt, 2023

ISBN 978 1 52678 245 8

The right of Danny Burt to be identified as Author of this work has been asserted by him in accordance with the Copyright, Designs and Patents Act 1988.

A CIP catalogue record for this book is available from the British Library All rights reserved.

No part of this book may be reproduced or transmitted in any form or by any means, electronic or mechanical including photocopying, recording or by any information storage and retrieval system, without permission from the Publisher in writing.

Printed and bound in India by Replika Press Pvt. Ltd.
Typeset in Ehrhardt MT Std 11.5/14 by
SJmagic DESIGN SERVICES, India.

Pen & Sword Books Ltd incorporates the imprints of Pen & Sword Archaeology, Air World Books, Atlas, Aviation, Battleground, Discovery, Family History, History, Maritime, Military, Naval, Politics, Social History, Transport, True Crime, Claymore Press, Frontline Books, Praetorian Press, Seaforth Publishing and White Owl

For a complete list of Pen & Sword titles please contact

PEN & SWORD BOOKS LIMITED
47 Church Street, Barnsley, South Yorkshire, S70 2AS, England
E-mail: enquiries@pen-and-sword.co.uk
Website: www.pen-and-sword.co.uk

Or
PEN AND SWORD BOOKS
1950 Lawrence Rd, Havertown, PA 19083, USA
E-mail: Uspen-and-sword@casematepublishers.com
Website: www.penandswordbooks.com

# Contents

| | | |
|---|---|---|
| *Acknowledgements* | | vi |
| *Introduction* | | vii |
| *Foreword by Wing Commander 'D-Reg' Bhasin MBE, RAF* | | ix |
| *In Memory* | | xi |
| Chapter 1 | History of the Iraq Air War – Op Granby | 1 |
| Chapter 2 | Gulf War Jaguar Performance and Upgrades | 4 |
| Chapter 3 | Operations Record Book January–February 1991 (RAF 540) | 12 |
| Chapter 4 | Pilots' Personal Extracts | 44 |
| Chapter 5 | Squadron Ground Crew | 142 |
| *Epilogue* | | 153 |
| *Appendix I* | *Jaguar Nose Art* | 156 |
| *Appendix II* | *Sorties Flown 17 January–27 February 1991* | 173 |
| *Appendix III* | *Aircraft Loadout* | 174 |
| *Appendix IV* | *Mission Data* | 175 |
| *Appendix V* | *EMI Recce Pod* | 176 |
| *Appendix VI* | *Gulf War Newspaper Article* | 180 |
| *Appendix VII* | *Ground Liaison Officer* | 184 |
| *Appendix VIII* | *Jaguar – Gulf War Twenty-Minute Presentation* | 187 |
| *Appendix IX* | *Surviving Gulf War Jaguars* | 199 |
| *Appendix X* | *Recovery of Jaguar GR1B XX962 'Fat Slags'* | 204 |
| *Appendix XI* | *Operational Awards* | 207 |
| *Appendix XII* | *Abbreviations* | 211 |
| *Index* | | 214 |

# Acknowledgements

This book has been a pleasure to document and the outcome has only been possible thanks to the assistance and encouragement so kindly provided by the various people and departments who have gone out of their way to help and answer the many questions I have asked them.

I would like to thank my partner, Erica, to whom I owe my sincere love and thanks. Second to the 'leader', Wing Commander Frankie Buchler, my senior instructor on my Typhoon Qualified Weapons Instructors course, who flew this amazing aircraft when he was a junior pilot all those years ago. Also, Squadron Leader Dheeraj Bhasin, 'D-Reg', and Squadron Leader Ian Smith, ex Jag mates, must get a mention for their support and interest.

In no set order, all the pilots who have taken time to write their memories down on paper, taking time out of their busy lives and to invite me into their private worlds. I will not mention them by name here as their stories are told in great detail in this book. The families of these pilots must be recognised, and they have shared their emotions and memories of when their loved ones were on dangerous military operations.

I would also like to recognise the members of the ground crew who kept these amazing aircraft flying for the duration of the deployment. Relying on basic equipment and in high humid conditions, it is a credit to the skill and professional commitment these men and women displayed.

Invaluable help came from the Air Historical Branch and the RAF Museum Hendon, answering and helping with my research questions via email and post. All applicable RAF squadrons and their respective associations for providing a great depth of detail and information from an extensive library and network of paperwork and records. RAF Pembrey Sands Air Weapons range and its DIO staff for helping me to recover and rescue an important part of this specific historic military event.

My publisher, Pen and Sword, and Martin Mace, who has spent endless hours putting my complicated notes into some kind of structure, so it forms the basis of this book. Paul Farquharson, one of my JTACs, but also a 'ninja' on Photoshop, for bringing a lot of the poor-quality photos back to life. Many others have provided me with useful information; hopefully, I have acknowledged their help, either by footnote, or by direct reference in their appropriate summary. Thus, for any omissions on my part, I hereby humbly apologise.

# Introduction

At the end of the Second World War and the turning point of military aviation, the propeller was replaced by the jet engine and the historic well-known aircraft such as the Spitfire and Lancaster were cast out to be cut up and destroyed for scrap. Over the decades their pilots, crews and ground engineers have departed this world due to age beating them, and the few still with us find their memory fades and it is hard for them to to recall their tales of air combat, and the key role that they played as part of the RAF, flying in combat missions against a real enemy. To them their memories of that time did not mean anything apart from it just being their normal life, but it is actually part of our country's important military history; a glimpse, a snapshot into a time that has gone by.

Gulf War 1, now thirty years past, is only now becoming embraced into that history. The RAF played a vital role in the air campaign when the coalition forces led attacks on Iraqi military targets commencing in mid-January 1991. The kinetic strike missions to interdict and destroy enemy lines of communication carried out by the RAF were initially planned to be at low level, for which the Jaguar was the perfect aircraft and completed a total of 618 combat sorties in forty-two days without the loss of any aircrew. In addition, the important combined effort of the RAF Tornado and Buccaneer force performed with similar outstanding success and this must not be forgotten. Both accumulated a mass of combat operational flying hours and both have their own stories to tell.

My personal ambition and desire is to record in detail all this information about an air conflict that military historians or the generic reader knows little about. Within this book there is some overlap, with some pilots talking about the same combat mission but from their own viewpoint and memories. However, I feel this book details what the RAF, particularly the Jaguar force, achieved with such limited time and resources to prepare for war fighting and how it continues to teach us the modern methods of warfare techniques. From this conflict many lessons were learned that were employed in the RAF's continuing role over the Balkans and Syria, from enforcing no-fly zones to its employment and deterrent against Islamic State today.

It leaves me to urge you to enjoy this book and learn about what a small bunch of people did in a small amount of time and made their small mark in history!

Danny Burt

*'I have seen in your eyes a fire of determination to get this war job done quickly. My confidence in you is total, our cause is just. Now you must be the thunder and lightning of Desert Storm.'*

General Norman Schwarzkopf

# Foreword

## By Wing Commander 'D-Reg' Bhasin, MBE, RAF

It is the greatest privilege to be able to write the foreword to this book. It is a rare piece of work that combines both factual and personal accounts from an era that defines the modern Royal Air Force, and the transition of warfare from the Cold War era to the more modern Expeditionary era, that is characterised by a new generation of flexibility, mobility and firepower. It beautifully combines actual records, real-world information, and the humanity of life on combat operations – the fear, the fortitude and the humour. It is the best tribute to the women and men of the Jaguar Force that I have read – it will be profoundly evocative for those who were there; and for those, like me, who subsequently flew the aircraft, and it will be supremely educational for the interested reader. What you read here is how it actually happened.

The Jaguar was not a particularly iconic aeroplane – it did not have swing wings, and it was not a jump jet. It did not have stunning performance; nor at the time was it great at night, or in bad weather, or with precision-guided munitions. If you mishandled it, it would kill you without even a warning. But what it *was* capable of delivering was quiet competence; brought about by simplicity and reliability, almost superhuman skill and knowledge of those who kept it flying, and careful and detailed selection and training of the pilots. No pilot of any more capable aeroplane would deny how this aircraft punched above its weight.

The Jaguar made its operators work for a living. The hard work that was put into the aircraft by all involved, combined with the relatively small size of the Force, created an *esprit de corps* and cohesion rarely seen in an organisation that is nevertheless defined by those characteristics. It is testament to that cohesion that, thirteen years after the disbandment of the force, and thirty years after the first Gulf War, the Jaguar family is still alive and well – meeting up in a series of reunions, keeping in touch via all sorts of media, and honouring the history of the Force and the aircraft. It is the greatest privilege to have been part of this incredibly special and unique Band of Brothers.

The pilots mentioned in this book are the heroes of my life. I know the majority of them; I have flown with them – and their example to me, their training of me, and their investment in me has defined me as a professional aviator and war fighter. The first Gulf War was the most intense fighting that the Jaguar Force ever saw, and our nation could not have asked for more from the 'few' that went out there with the Jaguar.

Not only did they display the highest levels of professionalism, courage and discipline; they also showed humility, integrity and humanity. These men are disarming when you meet them – appearing normal, jovial and a little bit fallible. This book, though, demonstrates what they are really made of – a subject that they are unlikely to enter into themselves, as they are modest to a fault.

But not one of us who flew the Jaguar, or any other aeroplane, would be alive today without the engineers. When you are busily signing for an aeroplane from the engineers, or doing your walk around with the engineers, or strapping in with the engineer's help, or handing back the aircraft to the engineers after the sortie, you're in a haze of thought and mental rehearsal, and on a ±five-second timeline; and it's hard to notice and give due recognition for the care that they take over you and their aircraft. Only in the cold light of day, and after much reflection, do I realise the complexity, the detail, and the consequences of failure that these young, enthusiastic, and capable people were dealing with. And in the case of the first Gulf War, they were doing this in constantly changing circumstances, in fearful heat, and under the threat of missile attack at any time. Bravo, the engineers; and thank you.

Some of the people in this book are no longer with us in body, but they live on in our hearts, in our memories, and in the example that we follow as their successors. We will remember them in, and through, everything we do.

And so, to the author. I know him as being the most credible military operator in his field. Now I know him as a diligent researcher, a keen aficionado of the aircraft, the era and its people; and as someone who has some pretty spectacular reach in getting the material and the interviews that he got in order to write this book. He has encapsulated exceptionally well this most important conflict, which taught us so much, and he has showcased the fortitude of those who were involved. That fortitude, and those people, must not be forgotten, and so I offer my personal thanks to the author for his tireless work in producing this book. Any reader will be enthralled by the story he tells, and the history that he has immortalised.

# In Memory

*'Those that still have their stories to tell'*

Flight Lieutenant Roger Crowder standing beside Jaguar XZ364 'Saddam'. (*Courtesy M. Rainier*)

Flight Lieutenant Steve Shutt standing beside Jaguar XX725 'Johnny Fartpants', taken at RAF Akrotiri, Cyprus, en route back to the UK on the 'leopard trail' – as the long journey from Bahrain was named – on completion of combat operations. (*Source unknown*)

xii  Desert Cats: The RAF's Jaguar Force in the First Gulf War

Group Captain Mike Seares MBE. Passed away on 24 August 2005 (Extract included)

Flight Lieutenant Jon Marsden (left). Killed on a training sortie 12 September 1990, flew into the sea low-level in the Solway Firth, 5 miles off Southerness Point, Dumfries & Galloway, Scotland, flying Jaguar GR1A XZ387.

Flight Lieutenant Keith Collister. Killed on a training sortie 13 November 1990, Qatar, flying Jaguar GR1A XX754.

There are a number of Jaguar pilots who flew during this conflict who, due to personal reflection, decided not contribute to this book. I would like to acknowledge them as they are very much part of this book.

## Contributors

*Above left and above right*: Flying Officer Nick Collins, aka the 'big bopper'. (*Courtesy W. Pixton and M. Rainer*)

Flight Lieutenant Dave Foote (Footy) preparing for a sortie in Jaguar XX725 'Johnny Fartpants'. (*Courtesy M. Rainer*)

Piloting Jaguar XZ119 'Katrina Jane', believed to be at the end of hostilities on a training sortie. (*Courtesy A. Emtage*)

*Above*: A unofficial badge that originated from the USAF Reno Air National Guard, who were based at Sheikh Isa Bahraini Air Force base during the Gulf War conflict. They designed and distributed the badge, which included the Jaguar force. (*Courtesy D. Bagshaw*)

*Above left*: Flight Lieutenant Craig Hill seated in Jaguar XZ118 'Buster Gonad'. (*Courtesy 41 Sqn, RAF*)

*Above right*: Flight Lieutenant Richard 'Dick' MacCormac conducting a 'walk around' of an unidentified Jaguar. (*Courtesy 41 Sqn, RAF*)

*Chapter 1*

# History of the Iraq Air War – Op Granby

Op Granby was the operational name given to the British mission in the Iraq war, sitting second to the US's overarching name of Desert Storm. The name came from John Manners, Marquess of Granby, a British commander in the Seven Years' War of 1756–63 between every major nation spanning five continents.

On 2 August 1990 Iraq invaded Kuwait. The international community was outraged, and immediate economic sanctions were brought to bear on Iraq by the UN Security Council. Initially the United States sent a large military force to Saudi Arabia and the US President, George Bush, urged other nations to send military forces to join and form a coalition. This collective force became the largest since the Second World War. On 29 November 1990, the United Nations Security Council Resolution 678 was established that gave Iraq until 15 January 1991 to withdraw all troops from Kuwait. Empowered states were directed to use 'all necessary means' if Iraq did not meet this deadline. Iraq chose to ignore this resolution and the build-up of Western military powers on their borders.

Overarching command of the Gulf War air mission was assumed by Lieutenant General Chuck Horner, USAF, Commander and Chief of the forward US Central Command, while General Norman Schwarzkopf remained in the United States. British command was based at Riyadh, the Joint Allied Headquarters, initially under Air Vice Marshal Andrew Wilson from 1 October–17 November 1990. He was succeeded by Air Vice Marshal William Wratten until the cessation of hostilities, with aircraft now almost totally integrated into a single coalition force. The air campaign was largely finished by 23 February 1991, when the coalition invasion of Kuwait took place. The primary mission of the RAF was to prevent the Iraqi Air Force from operating to any significant degree to attack coalition troops.

On 17 January 1991 Operation Desert Storm was launched, consisting of more than 1,000 combat sorties a day. The aerial strike force was made up of more than 2,250 coalition combat aircraft, which included 1,800 US aircraft.

On the morning of 17 January at 0238hrs (Baghdad time), Task Force Normandy, consisting of eight US Army AH-64 and two MH-53 Pave Low Helicopters, successfully engaged and destroyed Iraqi early warning radar systems on the Iraq–Saudi Arabia border. At 0243hrs the main strike package consisting of two USAF EF-111 Ravens with terrain-following radar led twenty-two USAF F-15E Strike Eagles in attacks on airfields in western Iraq. EF-111 crew Captain James Denton and Captain Brent

Brandon destroyed an Iraqi Dassault Mirage F1 when their low-altitude manoeuvring led the fighter to crash.

Between 17 January 1991 and 23 February 1991 an extensive 'Joint' air bombing phase was conducted, with the coalition flying more than 100,000 sorties. A huge amount of ordnance amounting to 88,500 tons was dropped, destroying not only military targets but a large amount of civilian infrastructure. The attacks included seven B-52s, which flew a thirty-four-hour nonstop, 14,000-mile round-trip from Barksdale Air Force Base and launched thirteen AGM-86 ALCM cruise missiles against Iraqi targets. The Iraqi force of 934 combat aircraft, of which 550 were operational, included Soviet types and French Mirage F1 fighters.

Most coalition sorties were launched from Saudi Arabia and the six coalition aircraft carriers in the Persian Gulf and Red Sea. Persian Gulf carrier battle groups (CVBGs) included USS *Midway*, *Theodore Roosevelt* and *Ranger*. USS *America*, *John F. Kennedy* and *Saratoga* operated from the Red Sea, with *America* transitioning to the Persian Gulf midway through the air war.

A primary concern was the Scud sites, media hubs, airfields and command centres located deep in the countries, both Iraq and Kuwait. These were viewed as high pay-off targets and would be destroyed using BGM-109 Tomahawk cruise missiles launched from warships situated in the Persian Gulf, F-117A Nighthawk stealth bombers with an armament of laser-guided smart bombs, and F-4G Wild Weasel aircraft armed with HARM anti-radar missiles. This allowed fighter-bombers to gain air superiority over the country and then continue to drop TV and laser-guided bombs onto specific pre-planned targets. Ten USAF F-117 Nighthawk stealth bombers, under the protection of three EF-111s, also bombed Baghdad. This formation came under fire from 3,000 anti-aircraft guns on the ground.

These attacks were co-ordinated with RAF missions and within twenty-four hours, 100 sorties had been completed. After seven days, the RAF's focus, like the rest of the coalition air forces, moved to targets related to the support of Iraqi forces in Kuwait. These included oil refineries and strategic bridges over the River Euphrates.

Iraqi leader Saddam Hussein tried to keep the morale of his forces and country high and stated, 'The great duel, the mother of all battles has begun. The dawn of victory nears as this great showdown begins.'

Iraq lost a total of 259 aircraft, 105 of which were lost in combat. During Desert Storm, thirty-six Iraqi aircraft were shot down in aerial combat, while three helicopters and two fighters were shot down during the invasion of Kuwait on 2 August 1990. Kuwait claims to have shot down as many as thirty-seven Iraqi aircraft, although these claims have not been confirmed. In addition, sixty-eight fixed-wing aircraft and thirteen helicopters were destroyed on the ground, and 137 aircraft were flown to Iran and never returned.

The coalition lost a total of seventy-five aircraft – fifty-two fixed-wing and twenty-three helicopters – during Desert Storm, with thirty-nine fixed-wing aircraft and five helicopters actually lost in combat. One coalition fighter was lost in air-to-air combat, a US Navy F/A-18. Unconfirmed Iraqi aerial victory claims including an RAF Tornado GR1A. However, the Tornado in question crashed to the ground due to pilot error on a different date than the supposed air-to-air kill is claimed to have taken place. One B-52G was lost while returning to its operating base on Diego Garcia when it suffered a catastrophic electrical failure and crashed into the Indian Ocean, killing three of the six crew. The rest of the coalition losses came from anti-aircraft fire. The Americans lost twenty-eight fixed-wing aircraft and fifteen helicopters; the British lost seven fixed-wing aircraft; the Saudi Arabians lost two; the Italians lost one; and the Kuwaitis lost one. During the Iraqi invasion of Kuwait on 2 August 1990, the Kuwaiti Air Force lost twelve fixed-wing aircraft, which were destroyed on the ground, and eight helicopters, six of which were shot down and two of which were destroyed while on the ground. Only forty-two of all these losses were the result of Iraqi action, with the other thirty-three due to accidents. In particular, RAF and US Navy aircraft that flew at low altitudes to avoid radar were particularly vulnerable, although this changed when the aircrews were permitted to fly above the anti-aircraft artillery (AAA).

This conflict was the first of its kind using GPS precision and advanced computer-guided weapons and munitions, even though these were very much in the minority when compared with 'dumb bombs' used. Cluster munitions and BLU-82 'Daisy Cutters' were heavily utilised during this period. Due to these types of weapons being used a comprehensive assessment of collateral and civilian casualties was made. Coalition bombing raids destroyed major Iraqi civilian infrastructure, with eleven out of twenty major power stations and 119 substations totally destroyed, with a further six power stations damaged. At the end of the war, electricity production was at 4 per cent of its pre-war levels. Bombs destroyed all major dams, most major pumping stations and many sewage treatment plants. Telecommunications equipment, port facilities, oil refineries, railways and bridges were also destroyed. Iraqi media used this to their advantage and often reported speculative claims to the worldwide audience, an example being when coalition aircraft apparently attacked the holy cities of Najaf and Karbala and killed 2,278 civilians, with a further 5,965 reportedly wounded.

It was unoffically documented that RAF aircrews were frustrated by the lack of combat and the heavy restraints that were placed on them by modern legal rules of engagement and collateral concerns. The quality of equipment was also questioned. As it had been a hasty deployment, sufficient financial support was not in place to sustain a modern warfare operation for an extended period of time. At the end of the conflict it was realised that the United Kingdom needed to modernise its military in certain areas.

*Chapter 2*

# Gulf War Jaguar Performance and Upgrades

Twelve GR1A Jaguar aircraft took part in the 1990-91 Gulf War, taking off from RAF Coltsihall, Norfolk, and arriving in two waves, with the first seven aircraft arriving at Thumrait, Oman, on 23 October, and the remaining five arrived on 2 November as part of the 41 Squadron roulemont. All these aircraft had been modified to what was to become known as 'Granby Stage 3' upgrades, this being a hasty upgrade. The official title given to this RAF modification programme was known as 'Fast Track', although some of the ground crew nicknamed this more appropriately 'Operation Goalpost', due to the MoD's decision-making and the size of the work to be carried out.

Newly designed Rolls-Royce Adour Mk104 turbofans were fitted, with better performance including thrust and, conveniently, improved higher turbine temperatures. Being a twin-engine aircraft, the Jaguar had enhanced survivability if an engine was damaged as it could still operate on a single one. Engine changes could be completed by competent ground crew within thirty minutes!

The first significant change to the Granby Stage 3 Jaguar was the paint scheme. Traditionally the Jaguar was painted either in a disruptive camouflaged pattern or alkaline removable temporary finish (ARTF) light grey. The first Jaguar detachment that deployed to the Gulf in August 1990 with 6 Squadron featured aircraft painted in

Jaguar XZ358 'Diplomatic Service' displaying her two rear-engine exhausts. (*Courtesy N. Weight*)

a unique ARTF Desert Sand. This specific paint scheme was designed for low-level operations by Philip Barley at the Royal Aircraft Establishment. Ten aircraft were painted in a record time of five hours (!) the day before flying out to Oman to start operations. This was undertaken with help from Air Cadets, who were at that time on their annual summer camp at Coltishall. This colour was adopted for the 41 Squadron roulemont.

Further modifications included the wing leading edges, which were treated with surface wave radar-absorbent material (SWAM), and radar-absorbent material (RAM) tiles fitted to the engine intakes to help reduce radar cross section. A film of gold coating was also added to the canopy to limit radar signature.

The next significant upgrade was the Sky Guardian 200-13PD RWR, replacing the ageing AR1-18223 RHWR, a pulse-Doppler radar processor-controlled crystal video RWR, covering E to J radar frequency bands with the option for C/D and R bands to be added. This could scan and identify targets at ranges in depth.

A Ferranti ARI23231 LRMTS had previously been mounted in the nose, giving the GR1 a 'chisel nose' appearance. As part of the Granby stage 3 upgrade a Mk XII Mode 4 IFF was added, consisting of an interrogation encoded pulse chain similar to the one used in previous models. The receiver side of the transponder would check the code against a known day code, and only respond if the two matched. The pulses in the reply were delayed based on the received code. This largely eliminated the ability of the enemy to trigger the transponder.

Already housed in the cockpit was the Ferranti FIN 1064 navigation system, featuring an inertial navigation system, plus a new computer and power supply, in place of the NAVWASS. The FIN 1064 was much more compact than NAVWASS, with one black box replacing five, and was far more accurate and capable. Mission data could be programmed into the FIN 1064 by plugging in a memory module.

For countermeasures, the Westinghouse AN/ALQ-101 (V)-10 noise deception jammer was added, a by-product from the US military during the Vietnam conflict. It was initially designed to cover the lower frequencies – in this case as E, F, G and H bands – but was expanded to cover I and J bands. The designers ran out of internal space, so a lower 'gondola' section was added to the lower surface of the 10in-diameter pod. A Phimat chaff pod and twin Tracor AN/ALE-40 Counter Measure Dispenser System (CMDS) were added and upgraded to fire both Type 118 and M206 flares. This provided the means by which the pilot could release chaff or flare, depending on the threat type, to counter any homing of a missile onto the plane. Chaff is a very simple yet effective system that consists of millions of tiny strands of aluminium foil and each strip is cut to length to match the various wavelengths of the radar. The flares had a longer burn time and were configured to be fired even if the undercarriage was lowered. Jaguars usually operated in flights of four, with two aircraft carrying jammer pods and two carrying Sidewinders.

Communication systems were also upgraded. A Magnavox AN/ARC-164 Have Quick, frequency-hopping radio was added with a distinctive large, single T-blade

6  Desert Cats: The RAF's Jaguar Force in the First Gulf War

antenna fitted to the external spine of the aircraft replacing the VHF twin fit. However, it is interesting to note that the legacy HF communications that remained fitted in the cockpit aided many combat missions.

Squadron Leader Mike Gordon recalls:

> Having an army GLO [ground liaison officer] with us, he thought of things we didn't. He had brought with him an HF radio. The Jaguar was one of the few aircraft left in the world that had a HF radio fitted in it. Most of the recce pilots

*Above and below*: Jaguars XX748 and XZ375 'The Guardian Reader' at dispersal, fitted with over-wing AIM-9L missiles. External fuel tanks are fitted to the centre line, as is the distinctive rear-mounted cockpit single-line T-shape UHF blade antenna. (*Courtesy N. Weight*)

used this on a daily basis. We would send our Misreps back to Headquarters via bouncing the signal, getting a hone patch from one of our listening sites back to base. Therefore, it was natural to us. Everyone was scrabbling around for radios and we were using one of the only radios that nobody could intercept.

The Jaguar's lethal combat capability consisted of two internally housed Royal Small Arms Mark 4 30mm Aden cannon with a capacity of 150 rounds in each gun bay. Over-wing AIM-9L Sidewinder pylons were fitted, designed by Jaguar International. This was a hasty modification carried out by the Sultan of Oman Armed Forces (SOAF). Over-wing air-to-air missiles were first fitted to RAF aircraft that were originally supplied to India, but not the GR1A. This AAM trial had been completed at A&AEE Boscombe Down in September 1990 on Jaguar XZ385 of 54 Squadron, being approved for operational service within one week!

When the Jaguar was initially deployed on combat operations the standard conventional loadout of four 1,000 GP bombs were carried. With some of this weaponry of Second World War vintage and with bombs being dropped frequently, fuses began to be in short supply, as Flight Lieutenant Mark Hopkins recalls:

> We came in one morning and Bill [Pixton] asked if anyone had used what was known as pistol fuses. There was a card made of something and a vial of acid.

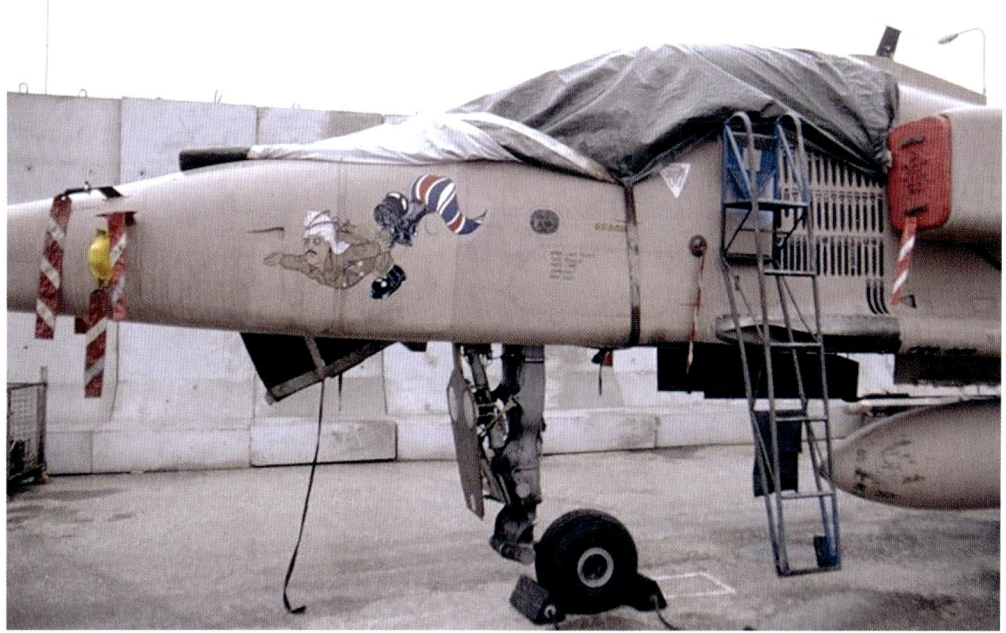

Jaguar XZ364 'Saddam' at dispersal. The port-side 30mm Aden cannon shroud is clearly visible behind the cockpit ladder (*Courtesy M. Rainer*)

You punched it and how long it would take to work through the card was the delay. They had been taken out of service years before. The Tornado had the brand new fuses, but we were using the old 947s, 951s, 952s. We then ended up using these pistol fuses. Bill was the only person who had flown with these. By the end of the war we were 45 degree dive tipping in from 30,000ft. The thing you had to watch out for is when you tipped in you throttled right back otherwise the weapons would come off almost supersonic.

The type of fuses that were fitted to these bombs were often witnessed by pilots to be unpredictable and it was not uncommon for them to pre-detonate.
Flight Lieutenants Toby Craig and Dick MacCormac commented on a similar experience when a pre-detonation occurred on 24 January as part of Keeper 01 Flight during a combat mission. Their target consisted of a mix of a Silkworm site and M46 artillery.
Flight Lieutenant Craig:

I tipped in the dive behind him, I remember going down the dive and there was this explosion. I remember saying the flak was a bit heavy today. Actually, when we looked at the film afterwards it was his weapons fusing on each other. The 952 fuse, if it sensed another weapon, they would explode. We were doing 20 degree dives with 947s.

Flight Lieutenant MacCormac:

What I remember about that trip was an extraordinarily large (compared to the AAA we were used to) orange, black-trimmed explosion some way in front of *my* aircraft. No idea what it was at the time and I didn't dwell on it – it was not a factor, and I was well into the dive and busy with the attack. At the debrief, though, those in the four-ship behind me discussed a similar event behind me. They had initially thought it was massive AAA, before concluding that it was one of my bombs detonating in mid-air, probably at the point of arming. The point of this is that I saw a similar prem-det [premature detonation]. Meaning that several of the 952-fused bombs went off the same way; not just mine. To my recollection, I was behind Toby Craig, and I assume, therefore, that the explosion I saw was one of *his* bombs. Much later, Mike Seares and I talked about the 'why' of this and came to some possible conclusions, but that's probably out of scope.

Other weapon upgrades included Canadian-manufactured CRV-7 70mm unguided rocket pods, as well the US-built CBU-87 Combined Effects Munition (CEM), although since these were longer than the traditional British BL-755 cluster bombs only one could be fitted on a pylon; two BL-755s could be carried in tandem.

All this extra weaponry, external fuel tanks and pods of various descriptions 'bolted' onto the Jaguar caused an excessive amount of extra weight on the aircraft, being able to carry a total of 4,765kg (10,500lb) of stores. Flight Lieutenant Toby Craig recalls the resulting performance in combat when heavily laden:

> It was quite terrible. It was an aircraft designed for flying around 50ft, not 20,000ft. So fully armed we could get to 20,000ft in dry heat, no problem. We often would go to 25,000ft–28,000ft and we needed afterburner to get up there. A little partial throttle reheat. Once you got up there you could stay there, there was no manoeuvre at high altitude. If you manoeuvre you lose speed and if you lose speed you fall out of the skies with no energy left. If you manoeuvred it too aggressively you ran the risk of blowing out the engine. Or you could have a little pop surge; you would hear this almighty bang. And then you had to check the engine instruments to see if you were in lock surge or it was just a little cough. Careful handling!

Over-wing AIM-9 Sidewinders fitted onto storage racks waiting to be loaded on Jaguars. (*Courtesy A. Emtage*)

## Specification

Engine propulsion: Two Rolls-Royce/Turbomeca Adour Mk104 engines

Engine power (each) dry/with afterburner: Operating temperature 700°C/725°C capable of about 5,500kgf dry and 8,000lb with max A/B (static)

Hardpoints: Eight

Speed: 1,699km/h/917kts/1,055mph

Service ceiling: 13.779m/45,207ft

Range: 528 miles/850km/458nm

Empty weight: 16.976lb/7.700kg

Max take-off weight: 15.700kg/34.613lb

Length: 55.22ft/16.83m

Width: 28.51ft/8.69m

Height: 16.04ft/4.89m

The internal cockpit layout of the upgraded Stage 3 GR1 Jaguar. These included unofficial modifications to prevent 'Pansy Pickles', where the bombs do not release. Seen in the first picture is the trigger mechanism on the top of the control stick. A safety guard was originally fitted over the weapon release switch but pilots' flying gloves would often get stuck under this flap and stop the release of weapons. It was removed by hacksaw via an 'in-house' modification. (*Authors collection*)

An unofficial in theatre modification to the Stage 3 Jaguar aircraft was a false canopy that was painted matt black onto the bottom of the cockpit area of the aircraft, this done to confuse potential threats to what type of aircraft this actually was. (*Courtesy of USAF*)

*Chapter 3*

# Operations Record Book January–February 1991 (RAF 540)

The outbreak of hostilities against Iraq on 16 January included the early involvement of the Jaguar detachment. By the end of the month 130 missions had been tasked, of which 110 were flown. The first week of hostilities was hampered by poor weather in the target area and led to several aborted missions.

Restrictions on the dropping of weapons on unplanned targets within Kuwait led to the planning of alternate targets. This ensured a high success rate when the poor weather prevented missions reaching their primary targets. Early missions showed unforeseen problems with weapon aiming and release during high-angle bombing in a high-threat environment.

Modifications to HUD symbology to help the pilots assess time to bomb release have been requested to alleviate this problem. As the weather improved so too did the imagery of the target area both from the intelligence network and from the on board HUD video. This allowed mission leader sufficient information to ensure minimum risk routing to their target areas. The HUD video has proved to be invaluable to confirm mission successes. Throughout the month the unit continued to react to missile raids, which after 16 Jan became a nightly occurrence, with 31 Scud missiles being directed into the eastern sector of the Arabian Peninsula. The use of the CRV-7 rocket pod in support of operations over the Arabian Gulf showed the necessity for a computer sight and CTTO (Central Trials and Tactics Organisation) were tasked with solving the problem, with gunsight software being produced by GEC (General Electric Company) Ferranti at Edinburgh.

A detailed breakdown of the unit operations since the outbreak of war is as follows:

## 16 Jan 91
No tasked missions but the unit was brought up to full war readiness.

## 17 Jan
1 × 4 ship tasked for CAS in the KTO. Mission lead entered Kill Zone without contact with control agency and chose command post as Tgt. 8 × 1000lb bombs in airburst mode were delivered with good results. A very successful mission showing the effectiveness of the war plan which allowed the formation into an area of intense air

A Jaguar taxiing from Muharraq on 17 January on the first combat mission of the Gulf War. (*Courtesy M. Cartwright*)

Squadron operations, L–R: Flight Lieutenant Roger Crowder, Stevie Thomas, Major Pat King (GLO), Flight Lieutenant Mike Seares (with camera). (*Courtesy M. Gordon*)

operations with no comms, yet deconflicted from other missions. The first RAF Jaguar war mission flown.

**18 Jan**
1 × 4 ship tasked with CAS in the KTO. 1 × a/c ground abort. The tasked Tgt was obscured by cloud so the formation redirected to their alternate Tgt. This was also in cloud, so Lead chose a known enemy position to release his weapons. The other a/c all returned to base with their weapons, partial mission success. 1 × 4 ship tasked with CAS in the KTO. In very poor weather all 4 a/c dropped bombs in Tgt area. AAA encountered in Tgt area.

A hand-held fire extinguisher in the squadron operations room. Note the phrase written on the pillar above. (*Courtesy M. Rainer*)

**19 Jan**
1 x ship tasked with AI in the KTO. In very poor weather all 8 a/c achieved their target, 2 × SA-2 sites. After a 40 minute transit in cloud the first 4 a/c attacked their site with airburst 1000lb bombs. The lead a/c could not release his bombs, but 12 bombs were released onto the target. The second 4 a/c delivered 16 bombs onto their target. The mission success was confirmed by the HUD video. All a/c encountered heavy AAA in the target area and on landing one a/c was found to have suffered minor flak damage. 1 × 4 ship tasked with AI in the KTO. 1 × air abort. In very poor weather the formation just managed to find the target area. The lead a/c could not identify the target, a GHN-45 Bty, and released his weapons on some support vehicles in scrapes south of the target. Number 2 did not release and number 4 released on the target with unknown results. 1 × 4 ship tasked with AI in KTO. In poor weather the lead and No 3 a/c identified their target, a MRL Bty, and released their weapons. The No 2 could not identify the target and flew to his pre-planned alternate but encountered even worse weather and aborted. Throughout the attack the formation encountered heavy, radar laid, AAA and on return 2 a/c were found to have minor flak damage.

**20 Jan**
1 × 8 ship tasked with AI in the KTO. The formation was split into 2 × 4s. The first 4 a/c found their target obscured in fog and aborted. The mission lead diverted the second 4 a/c to an alternate target but again weather precluded them identifying it. On leaving the target area the second 4 lead a/c identified an artillery position and released his weapons. On return to Muharraq airfield was out in fog and the formation diverted to Dhahran. 3 × 4 ships tasked with AI in the KTO. All cancelled due to weather in KTO.

**21 Jan**
2 × 8 ships tasked with AI in KTO. Both missions cancelled due to bad weather in the KTO.

**22 Jan**
2 × 6 ships tasked with AI in KTO. Both missions cancelled due to weather at Muharraq but the second was retasked as an 8 ship with later TOT. 1 × ground abort. The target, an ammunition storage area partially hidden below 4/8 of low CU cloud. 6 of the formation released weapons on the target and the other released on his alternate target. All a/c encountered AAA in the target area and several a/c received indications of SA-2 Acquisition radar. A successful mission in difficult weather conditions. 1 × 2 ship tasked with CSAR over the Gulf. The pair, fitted with 2 × CRV7 on each a/c, held CAP but were not used by their controlling agency 1 × 2 ship held on 30 min ground alert. Not used.

An unknown pilot preparing for a combat sortie in Jaguar XZ106 'Rule Britannia' armed with 1,000lb bombs on her tandem beam pylons. (*Courtesy RAF Copyright*)

## 23 Jan

1 × 8 ship tasked with AI in KTO. 2 × ground aborts. The six remaining a/c found their target, a D30 Arty and AAA site, and their 24 × 1000lb bombs were confirmed as impacting the Arty and AAA positions. The target was not at the position as tasked but a last minute update through the int network ensured a successful mission. All a/c encountered heavy AAA over the target area. 1 × 6 ship tasked with AI in KTO. The formation were to attack their target, an MRL Bty, 2 minutes after a package of USAF F16 a/c had attacked an airfield 3 miles to the east. During the attack one of the F16 a/c was shot down. The Jaguars pressed home their attack on their target with 4 a/c achieving direct hits and another releasing his weapons on his alternate target, some nearby artillery scrapes. 2 × 2 ship tasked on SUCAP over the Gulf. Both uneventful missions with no airborne tasking.

*Left and opposite*: Jaguar XX962 'Fat Slags' taking off from runway 030 at Muharraq. In the latter photo she is armed with CBU-87 CEMs. (*Courtesy A. Emtage and P. Tholen*)

**24 Jan**
1 × 8 ship tasked with AI in KTO. The formation was split into two with the first 4 × a/c targeting an M46 Arty Bty and the second 4 × a/c on a Frog 7 site. In excellent weather all a/c released onto the artillery position but because of a hang up only 3 × a/c released on the Frog 7 site. The formation encountered carpet AAA in the target area, fortunately below time. 1 × 4 ship tasked with AI in KTO. In excellent weather the formation achieved 2 direct hits on their target, a M46 Arty Bty. The No. 2 could not acquire the target as it was obscured by smoke from the leader's bombs so released on his alternate, a storage facility. The fourth a/c had problems with the computer sight in the HUD which has led the unit asking CTTO to make modifications to assist the pilots assess time to go to weapon release. 1 × 2 ship tasked on SUCAP over the Gulf. The first pair on SUCAP to be tasked. The pair vectored onto 2 inbound F1 Mirage a/c, with 15 miles to go they lost comms with the controlling AWACs, flew through the F1s and turned back towards their cap position. The 2 × F1s were dispatched by an F15 which then locked up the Jaguars. Fortunately, comms had been established with the AWACs controller that they were to break his lock. The formation lead then informed the AWACs controller that they were there for ground threats only and although they carried Sidewinders that they were only for self-defence and for pooping off at ground troops with gay abandon!! 1 × 2 ship tasked with SUCAP over the Gulf. An uneventful mission with only a visual ID on a helicopter and a sighting of a marine craft along the coast.

Jaguar XX962 'Fat Slags'. (*Courtesy A. Emtage*)

**25 Jan**
1 × 8 ship tasked with AI in KTO. Mission returned to base with weapons due to weather abort in the KTO. 1 × 4 ship tasked with AI in KTO. Mission returned to base with weapons due to weather abort in the KTO. 1 × 2 ship tasked with SUCAP over the Gulf. The formation were tasked with visual ID duties by controlling agency but unable to climb to FL440! The 2 a/c were then vectored onto a surface barge and cleared to engage. In conjunction with a USMC A-6, which marked the target, the pair released 4 × CRV7 rocket pods and 480 rounds of HE strafe. Hits were confirmed on the barge, but they were unable to sink it. During the attack the 2 a/c encountered light AAA from several small craft south of their target. 1 × 2 ship tasked with SUCAP over the Gulf. The 2 × a/c were vectored onto the same barge and released the same weapons as above. Hits were again confirmed but failed to sink the barge.

**26 Jan**
1 × 4 ship tasked with AI in KTO. The a/c found their target, a Silkworm site, in excellent weather. Damage assessment was confirmed visually and by HUD video after all weapons were released in the target area. The formation encountered AAA up to 10,000ft. 1 × 6 ship tasked with AI in KTO. 1 × ground abort. The formation found their target, a M46 Arty Bty, to be in three distinct groups. Weapons were released on all targets and the assessment was one site destroyed and the other two damaged. Several other artillery positions were seen in the target area and details were passed to the target co-ordinators. 1 × 2 ship tasked with SUCAP over the Gulf. An uneventful mission with the pair being vectored onto a surface vessel which could not be identified as hostile. The a/c returned with all weapons. 1 × 2 ship tasked with SUCAP over the Gulf. Mission was cancelled on ground by higher authority.

Operations Record Book January–February 1991 (RAF 540)   19

Jaguar XZ119 'Katrina Jane' preparing to taxi. (*Courtesy A. Emtage*)

## 27 Jan
1 × 8 ship tasked with AI in KTO. Mission returned with weapons after finding solid cloud to 25,000ft in the KTO. 1 × 4 ship tasked with AI in KTO. The first 2 a/c managed to identify their target, a Silkworm site, and released with four of the bombs confirmed as a direct hit on the site. The second 2 a/c elected to go to the alternate target, an ammunition storage site, and successfully released their weapons. 2 × 2 ship tasked with SUCAP over the Gulf. Missions were cancelled by higher authority.

## 28 Jan
1 × 8 ship tasked with AI in KTO. The target, a large barracks, was divided into 2 DMPIs for 2 × 4 ships. In excellent weather the lead and No 2 dropped their weapons on the target, assessed as direct hits by the No 3 and 4 who could not determine their DMPIs due to smoke from the first 8 bombs. They released onto their alternate target, a D30 Bty just to the south of the barracks. The second 4 × a/c released onto their target although 4 bombs were dropped well short due to an auto attack weapon release malfunction. A very successful mission with target damage assessed both visually and by HUD video. 1 × 4 ship tasked with AI in KTO. The target, a logistics site was achieved with few problems in excellent weather. The formation hit 4 DMPIs on the large site with MK 87 CBUs and damage was considerable with parts of the site on fire when the formation cleared the target area. The MK 87 CBU was found to be an ideal weapon for this type of target. 1 × 2 ship tasked on SUCAP over the Gulf. An uneventful mission with the pair being directed to a burning oil platform to give

Jaguar aircraft lined up in the concrete (parade) blast pens at dispersal. (*Courtesy M. Rainier*)

progress report. The pair returned to base with their weapons. 1 × 2 ship tasked with SUCAP over the Gulf. The only task asked of the pair was to check the identity of a surface vessel close to Kuwait City. The pair were en route but had to break off because of Mirage F1 activity in the area. The a/c returned to base with all weapons.

**29 Jan**
1 × 8 ship tasked with AI in KTO. 1 a/c ground abort. The seven remaining a/c achieved their target, 2 Silkworm missile sites. 1 a/c had indications of fighter lock up and missile launch. All a/c encountered light AAA fire in the target area. The results using MK 87 CBUs were assessed as damage to one sight and a DH on the second target. A good mission in excellent weather. 1 × 4 ship tasked on AI in the KTO. All four a/c achieved the target, a Silkworm site, using MK 87 CBUs. No AAA was encountered in the target area and results were assessed as damage to the western half of the site which included radar and support vehicles. During the return leg of the mission 4 × FPBs were sighted in the Gulf and their location passed to HMS Gloucester, a Naval Destroyer in the area. A fifth a/c was launched with this mission carrying the new LOROP camera to assess the recce potential for further missions. 2 × 2 ship tasked on SUCAP in the Gulf. As a result of the information from the above mission the first pair were vectored onto the 4 FPBs. There were 15 FPBs in total which the pair followed but were not allowed to engage. They were also vectored

Jaguar XZ358 'Diplomatic Service'. (*Courtesy M. Gordon*)

onto a partially sunken tanker for an update report for the Navy. The second pair, who were initially holding 30 min readiness, were scrambled to engage the FPBs which had now been declared as hostile. The pair attacked using 2 × CRV7 each with a follow up pass using HE strafe. Confirmation was later destroyed and 12 damaged. During the attacks both a/c encountered AAA.

**30 Jan**
1 × 8 ship tasked with AI in KTO. The 8 a/c found their target, a 2S1 Arty Bty, in thick haze and under 4/8 of CU with tops at 13,000ft. Target acquisition was difficult however the formation managed to drop 15 × MK 87 CBUs on their briefed DMPIs. 1 a/c had a hung bomb, which he attempted to release on the alternate target but was unable to due to poor weather. The weather conditions over the target precluded any damage assessment. 1 × 4 ship tasked with AI in KTO. The formation found their target, a command post, totally obscured by smoke with haze and returned to base without releasing their weapons. 1 × a/c fitted with the LOROP camera flew with the formation to carry out further trials. 1 × 2 ship on SUCAP over the Gulf. The pair were initially vectored onto a burning tanker to give an update report and then onto a maritime patrol a/c visually ID it. The a/c turned out to be a friendly P3 Orion. After refuelling the pair were vectored onto an Iraq Navy POLNOCHNY. The ship was reported to the controlling agency and clearance was given to engage. The vessel was on fire amidships and after releasing 4 × CRV7 pods and 480 rounds of HE strafe the vessel was seen to be on fire from end to end. 1 × 2 ship on SUCAP over the Gulf. An uneventful mission with no airborne tasking.

**31 Jan**
1 × 8 ship tasked with AI in KTO. The mission was given two targets, an ammunition site and nearby logistics site, and elected to put 4 a/c onto each with a mixture of 1000lb bombs and MK 87 CBUs. The ammunition site was very large, and the first 4 a/c concentrated their weapons onto the western side of the site. Three of the second 4 a/c released onto the logistic site while the fourth had to manoeuvre, releasing chaff, due to fighter lock up and missile guidance indications from his EW equipment. Having negated the threat, he managed to release his weapons on the ammunition storage site. 1 × 4 ship tasked with AI in KTO. A fifth a/c joined the mission, fitted with the LOROP camera, to continue the trials. The target, a Silkworm site, was found and 7x CBU87s were released onto the site. The lead a/c could not release one of his weapons due to an electrical fault. The formation encountered no enemy defences but were continually being locked up by friendly fighters, before, during and after being in the KTO even though the controlling AWACS had the mission on their screens throughout. 1 × 2 ship tasked with SUCAP over the Gulf. As soon as the pair were airborne the AWACS controller retasked them with CAS. Their target was to recce

Flight Lieutenant Steve Shutt seated in Jaguar XZ367 'Debbie/White Rose'. (*Courtesy C. Allam*)

a road, just over the border, for concentrations of armour moving south. Both a/c attacked vehicles on the road, using BL755 CBUs. The attack by the No 2 happened to coincide with an APC parked at the side of the road. The APC later to be confirmed as a ZSU-234! As the lead a/c returned for a re-attack he encountered a SAM, probably a SAM 7, as he pulled off the target, requiring him to perform a missile break and jettison his stores. Both a/c returned to base safely. 1 × 2 ship tasked with SUCAP over the Gulf. After a long, uneventful mission the pair were handed off to a AWACS for CAS. The lead a/c decided that as the golden sun was sinking slowly below the distant horizon, its crimson aura was not producing enough light and declined the offer and returned to base.

## Training

Training continued as in previous months up until 15 Jan. Low flying areas in Saudi Arabia were used for AAR and low level evasion training. The unit also took part in several exercise with the Royal Navy in the Gulf of Arabia to assist the RN in defensive training, these exercises being given the official title of WASEX, war at sea exercise. On one occasion a formation was asked for a special fly-by of HMS *London*, for a VIP passenger, a message of appreciation was later passed to the Squadron from Mr John Major, the Prime Minister. Splash firing with the Royal Navy continued to provide valuable training. The usual range slots at King Fahad range were utilised. The Crab Island range on Bahrain was cleared for release of the CRV7 rocket pod and suitable trials and training were carried out on Faisal range in Saudi Arabia.

## Attachments and Detachments
After the outbreak of war on 16 Jan it became necessary to increase the number of pilots on the unit. Two missions planners were sent from UK followed shortly after by three pilots from RAF Coltishall.

## Visits
On 1 Jan a select band of officers were invited to a cocktail party on HMS *Brazen*.

## Social
A very timely party was held on 11 Jan in the Al Afnah, the function suite of the Diplomat hotel, for all serving officers at RAF Muharraq. Over 150 people attended from all units involved in RAF Muharraq for what was the last party before the outbreak of war.

L–R: Flight Lieutenants Craig Hill, Steve Shutt wearing pith helmet, Flying Officer Nick Collins and Flight Lieutenant Pete Tholen. (*Courtesy P. Tholen*)

## February 1991
## Muharraq, Bahrain

## Operations

As the war against Iraq continued unabated the unit continued to be involved at the forefront of operations, using 1000lbs bombs, MK87 CBUs and CRV-7 rocket pods. The Jaguars have maintained their high mission rate with ever improving results.

A total of 119 missions were tasked of which 114 were flown. It became apparent, during the month, that the Jaguar was being used primarily to destroy the Iraqi Artillery threat, both towed and self-propelled. The abundance of prepared, revetted areas that were available to these forces made target acquisition difficult when trying to confirm enemy occupation of a specific site while in the final stages of a dive attack.

The chemical threat that these forces have posed made it essential that every mission was successful, and it became apparent that good photographic imagery of the sites was essential. The trial of the LOROP camera continued and it was found to produce excellent results when used in conjunction with the F126, enabling pilots to select occupied, revetted areas in the mission planning stages. The introduction of new software for the MK87 CBUs and CRV-7 rocket pod late in the month increased the flexibility and effectiveness of the Jaguars. A detailed breakdown of the operational missions flown follows:

### 1 Feb

1 × 8 ship tasked with AI in the KTO. 1 × ac ground abort. The remaining 7 ac all achieved their target, the Al Jaber airfield support area, in excellent weather. A total of 24 × 1000lb bombs and 4 × Mk87 CBUs were released onto the target with the result of major structural damage to most of the complex. The mission was also able to confirm the success of a Kuwait AF A4 attack onto the airfield hangars to the north of their DMPIs. All aircraft encountered light AAA up to 15,000ft. 1 × 3 ship tasked with AI in the KTO. 1 × ac fitted with LOROP camera for post attack assessment. The mission released their weapon, Mk 87 CBUs onto the target, a Silkworm site. It was assessed that, with only 2 ac, the site had been damaged but would require re-tasking. The LOROP pod, although producing excellent photographs, was found to be difficult to aim accurately and of little use for damage assessment. The mission lead saw muzzle flashes from the site during his attack but saw no flak in the air. 2 × 2 ac tasked with SUCAP over the Gulf. Both the missions were employed in convoy search duties but failed to find anything to engage. All ac returned to base with their weapons.

In the foreground are Flight Lieutenant Roger Crowder, with Squadron Leader Mike Rondot, next to the nosewheel. Flying Officer Mal Rainier is at the top of the ladder, with Flight Lieutenant Alex Emtage at the bottom. Flanked on the right of Flight Lieutenant Pete Tholen are Flight Lieutenants Bob Neilson, ops officer, Steve Shutt and Craig Hill. Far right is Wing Commander Bill Pixton. The Jaguar is XZ364 'Saddam'. (*Courtesy M. Rainer*)

**2 Feb**
1 × 8 ship tasked with AI in the KTO. The mission encountered a heavy barrage of AAA over the target, an ammunition storage area, 1 ac had to manoeuvre to avoid the flak and missed the target and another ac suffered a hang up. The other 6 ac released a total of 12 × Mk 87 CBUs onto the target. 1 × 5 ship tasked with AI in the KTO. 1 ac fitted with LOROP camera. The mission found their target, a silkworm site in an area of intense, friendly air activity. This together with the weather and very heavy AAA, resulted in the first three ac being unable to acquire the target. The No 4 managed to release his weapons, 2 × Mk 87 CBUs, onto the target and a direct hit was confirmed by the lead ac. En route to the target formation witnessed the scale of the CAS bombing being unleashed onto the Iraqi ground forces. 1 × 2 ship tasked with SUCAP over the Gulf. As soon as the pair were airborne they were vectored up to Jazirat Miskin Island to hold CSAR cap for a downed USMC A-6 ac. The island was believed to be heavily defended. In conjunction with the A-6 the pair released 8 × 1000lb bombs, in the airburst mode, with the leads seen to impact over a 6 gun AAA emplacement. Unfortunately, there was no sign of the USMC pilot. 1 × 2 ship tasked with SUCAP

Preparing for take-off. (*Courtesy M. Rainier*)

over the Gulf. Both ac returned to unit when the lead ac suffered a surged engine shortly into the mission.

**3 Feb**
1 × 8 ship tasked with AI in the KTO. The target was a Silkworm site split into a north and south side. The formation decided to split up into 2 × 4s. The first 4 ac delivered 12 airburst and 4 impact 1000lb bombs directly onto the north site. The site was visually confirmed to be destroyed with secondary explosions seen as they departed the target area. The second 4 ac received an update to the position of the radar on their site as they taxied. In good weather the formation delivered the 12 airburst and 4 impact 1000lb bombs onto the updated position which they were able to confirm as being occupied. The south site was visually assessed to have been destroyed. 1 × 4 ship tasked with AT in the KTO. The formation found their target, an Arty Bty, in haze. The lead ac was the only one to positively identify the target and released his weapons. The other 3 ac routed to their alternate targets, a silkworm site, to release their weapons. The No 4 ac suffered a hang up but was able to confirm that 4 airburst 1000lb bombs had exploded directly over the site followed by a direct hit from the 4 impact 1000lbs bombs of the No 2 and 3. 1 ac observed SA2 lockup indications en route to the target area. 2 × 2 ship tasked with SUCAP over the Gulf. Both pairs were solely for visually identifying surface vessels in the Gulf. All ac returned to base with weapons.

28  Desert Cats: The RAF's Jaguar Force in the First Gulf War

**4 Feb**
1 × 4 ship tasked with AI in the KTO. The formation had difficulty in locating their target, a large barracks and storage complex, due to haze and smoke up to 20000ft. 16 × 1000lb bombs were released onto the target and damage was visually assessed as severe to several buildings and storage areas within the complex. 1 × 4 ship tasked with AI in the KTO. In thick haze the formation managed to acquire their target, a barracks, and released 16 × 1000lb bombs causing severe damage. 1 × 4 ship tasked with AI in the KTO. The formation had difficulty in identifying their target, a III Corps Command Post, due to thick haze. Having located the target 16 × 1000lb bombs were released all impacting within 50ft of the DMPI. The formation all encountered AAA over the target and received indications of ZSU-234 Gun Dish acquisition radar. 2 × 2 ship tasked with SUCAP over the Gulf. The 2 pairs held cap for 2.5 hrs but were not used and returned to base with their weapons.

**5 Feb**
1 × 5 ship tasked with AI in the KTO. The target, a radio relay mast, was found in excellent weather. The formation released 20 × 1000lb airburst bombs onto the target and although one ac had problems with his weapon aiming which put his bombs short of target which was assessed to be severely damaged. All ac encountered light AAA up to 12000ft. 1 × 4 ship tanked with AI in the KTO. The formation had difficulty contacting any controlling agency en route to the target, a radio relay mast (as above). Having found the target 16 × 1000lb airburst bombs were released with the result of

A aerial shot of a Jaguar flying medium level with a full payload, the AIM-9L Sidewinder's pylons clearly denoted on the outer upper wings. (*Courtesy* T. Craig)

only 1 ac doing any damage to what remained of the mast. 1 × 4 ship tasked with AI in the KTO. The formation found the target area in poor weather, however, the target an Arty Bty, was not at the tasked location. Identification of further targets within the Kill Zone was very difficult and only 1 ac managed to release his weapons on an enemy position. The other 3 ac all returned to base with their weapons. 1 × 4 ship tasked with AI in the KTO. The formation again found no Arty Bty at the tasked area and elected targets of opportunity within the Kill Zone. A total of 16 × 1000lbs were released on AAA and revetted sites. The result of this and the previous mission was to ensure the latest intelligence was available during the mission planning to ensure the optimum chance of locating what is a highly mobile target.

**6 Feb**
1 × 8 ship tasked with AI in the KTO. The formation found the weather unfit as they crossed the Kuwait border and returned to base with weapons. 1 × 8 ship was tasked with AI in the KTO. The target, an Arty Bty, was very difficult to acquire due to thick haze in the target area. A total of 32 × 1000lb bombs were released onto the target with 1 ac selecting his alternative Arty Bty because of obstruction of the prime target. Several of the ac had indications of SA-2 search radar inbound the target area.

**7 Feb**
2 × 4 ships tasked with AI in the KTO. The target, a large Arty Bty deployment area, allowed the formation to split into 2 × 4s. The first 4 ac had trouble contacting the control agency prior to reaching Kuwait. The lead ac had problems identifying the DMPI while trying to deconflict his formation from 4 × F18s and 2 × AV8Bs and released his bombs on his alternate target, further Arty. The other 3 ac all achieved the prime target releasing 12 × 1000lb airburst and impact bombs. The second 4 ac consolidated the attack and released 14 × 1000lb bombs onto a different area of the Arty Bty. Unfortunately, 2 ac had kit problems which meant their bombs were slightly off target but the No 3 scored a direct hit which was confirmed by No 4's HUD video. 1 × 5 and 1 × 4 ship tasked with AI in the KTO. The mission were working to a very late TOT and arrived in the target area to find haze and a low sun. The target, an Arty Bty, was consequently very difficult to acquire. 8 of the ac released into the target area but battle damage was impossible to assess. The last ac returned to base with his weapons having been unable to identify the target. The mission was partial success and earlier TOTs were requested to alleviate the problems encountered.

**8 Feb**
1 × 4 ship tasked with AI in the KTO. The formation found their target, an Arty Bty, in excellent weather. Target acquisition was easy, and the formation could confirm that it was a target rich environment with 50% of the revetted sites occupied.

All 16 × 1000lb bombs were released with excellent results confirmed both visually and by the HUD video. 1 × 4 ship tasked with AI in the KTO. Targeted against the same Arty Bty as above the formation enjoyed the same weather conditions and the same success after releasing another 16 × 1000lb bombs onto deployed artillery. The success of this mission was put down to the weather and the receipt of the latest in theatre intelligence on enemy positions just prior to walking. 1 × 5 ship tasked with AI in the KTO. The formation experienced comms jamming en route but found the target, an Arty Bty, in excellent weather. They were able to confirm the positions were occupied and released 19 × 1000lbs. 1 ac suffered a hang up of 1 bomb. Battle damage was assessed visually as good. 1 × 4 ship tasked with AI in the KTO. In excellent weather the formation found difficulty in acquiring the target, an Arty Bty, because of the amount of bomb damage from previous missions. They each choose a different DMPI and released 16 × 1000lb to great effect. BDA was good confirmed both visually and by HUD video.

**9 Feb**
1 × 4 ship tasked with AI in the KTO. The formation found their target, a logistics site, after an uneventful transit. They released 8 × MK 87 CBUs into the compound although BDA was difficult due to smoke obscuring the target. During the attack the formation were able to confirm that their alternative target, a scrap yard, did contain military vehicles as intelligence had suggested. 1 × 5 ship tasked with AI in the KTO. The formation were targeted against artillery but having found nothing at the DMPI released 10 × Mk87 CBUs onto their alternative target, the scrap yard that had been confirmed as active by the previous formation. The excellent weather allowed the pilots to attain accurate release parameters with the result of severe damage being inflicted to the site. The formation experienced comms jamming on two of the control frequencies and reported a fire which appeared to be an attempt at smoke screening. 1 × 4 ship tasked with AI in the KTO. The target, an MRL Bty, was partially obscured by cloud making the delivery of Mk 87 CBUs very difficult. 2 ac managed to release onto the target but only assessed their effectiveness as possible damage to the Bty. 1 ac had a hang up and returned to base with his weapons and the other released his on his alternative, a Silkworm site, which he was able to confirm as active with support vehicles and possible missiles. 1 × 4 ship tasked with AI in the KTO. The formation experienced some problems contacting their control agency en route to the target, a MRL Bty, because of comms jamming. Cloud hampered the attack, and the formation all released their 8 × Mk87 CBUs onto a Command Post in the same location as the MRL Bty. BDA was impossible due to the cloud.

**10 Feb**
1 × 4 ship tasked with AI in the KTO. 1 × ground abort. A last minute intelligence update which changed the position of the target, an Arty Bty, ensured the formation

Jaguars XX725, 'Johnny Fartpants' and XZ119 'Katrina Jane' conducting a 'TV take-off', in which they kept low for the benefit of the media at the end of the runway. (*Courtesy A. Emtage*)

found a 'target rich environment'. A total of 6 × Mk 87 CBUs were released onto concentrated Arty position with the first 4 bombs being confirmed as direct hits. The weather was excellent, but the formation increased fires in the KTO acting as smoke screens. 1 × 4 ship tasked with AI in the KTO. This turned out to be a very straight forward mission to an old target, a Silkworm site, in excellent weather. The formation reported seeing flashes from AAA guns on the ground but no airbursts and released 8 × MK87 CBUs onto the site. 1 × 4 ship tasked with AI in the KTO. 1 × ground abort. The excellent weather ensured the formation was able to acquire their target, a Silkworm site, from over 50 miles. The lead ac encountered problems with his weapons aiming and dropped his bombs slightly short but 4 × MK 87 CBUs were released onto target.

## 11 Feb

1 × 4 ship tasked with AI in the KTO. The formation received some excellent recce photos of the target, an Astros II MRL Bty which allowed them to select accurate DMPIs. In excellent weather 8 × MK 87 CBUs were released with the result that the whole site was covered, confirmed both visually and by HUD video. A very successful mission. 1 × 4 ship tasked with AI in the KTO. 1 × preselected DMPIs of the target, an Astros II MRL Bty. Unfortunately, all the 6 × MK87 CBUs dropped short of the MRLs but did completely destroy the command and support vehicles. The formation again reported the increased use of oil fires to try and obscure ground positions.

2 × 4 ship tasked with AI in the KTO. Both formations tasked with the same target, an Astros II MRL Bty, but all turned back to base due to a marked deterioration in the weather. 1 × 2 ship tasked with recce in the KTO. After the success of a previous mission due to good recce photos a further attempt was made to use the LOROP camera. The first target was obscured by cloud and the second had partial cloud cover. Unfortunately, the F126 camera failed. Although a failed mission there was some room for hope in using the LOROP in the vertical mode in conjunction with the F126.

**12 Feb**
1 × 4 ship tasked with AI in the KTO. The formation found their target, an MRL Arty Bty, in excellent weather. Early target acquisition and accurate release parameters ensured that the 8 × MK 87 CBUs all landed on the site in the groove. The formation encountered barrage AAA in the target area between 10000 and 15000ft.

1 × 4 ship tasked with AI in the KTO. The formation found their target, an MRL Arty Bty, in excellent weather. As the lead ac was about to tip in he saw two friendly fighters below him. He delayed the tip in and was unable to acquire the target but located a AAA site and released his 4 × 1000lb bombs on it. The other 3 ac achieved 6 × 1000lb bombs onto the DMPI, due to weapon aiming problems and hang ups, 6 bombs were jettisoned into the sea on return to base. 1 × 4 ship tasked with AI in the KTO. The formation found their target, an MRL Arty Bty, in good weather. Amid AAA up to 15000ft the first 2 ac tipped in and released 8 × 1000lb bombs onto the target. The No 3 ac confirmed that all the bombs scored direct hits and seeing an active coastal AAA site in the target area elected to release his 2 × Mk 87 CBUs on it causing secondary explosions on the site. The No 4 ac released his 2 × MK87 CBUs onto primary target and caused secondary explosions that could still be seen from 60 miles as the formation returned to base. A very successful and satisfying mission. 1 × 4 ship tasked with AI in the KTO. The formation found their target, an MRL Bty, had already been attacked and was burning. They released their 8 × 1000lb and 4 MK 87 CBUs onto the target area with the result of a probable hit on a SSV park in some nearby woods and a definite hit on a petrol station adjacent to the target. 1 × 2 ship tasked with recce in the KTO. The pair covered 2 targets, an Arty position and a MRL Bty. Coverage of the Arty positions by both LOROP and the F126 confirmed that the guns had been moved and three new positions were located for the next day's missions. The MRL position was covered on only F126 but coverage was sufficient to confirm three new sites.

**13 Feb**
1 × 4 ship tasked with AI in the KTO. The formation were locked up by SA-2 on ingress to their target a Comms post near Kuwait International Airport. Target acquisition was difficult in poor weather, but they managed to release all 16 × 1000lb bombs onto

the target, BDA was impossible due to cloud during the recovery. 1 × 4 ship tasked with AI in the KTO. The target, an Arty Bty, was acquired in excellent weather. The lead ac released his manually, scoring a direct hit, on an alternate Arty position. The last 2 ac released 4 × MK 87 CBUs onto the primary site to great effect, the bombs seem to impact the gun positions. On return to base the control agency tried to vector the formation into a Kill Zone for CAS work, but lack of fuel made them decline the offer. 1 × 4 ship tasked with AI in the KTO. The formation all experienced AAA on crossing the coast ingressing to the target, an MRL Bty. Target acquisition was easy in excellent weather, but the results achieved after releasing 8 × MK 87 CBUs were disappointing due mainly to no laser locks from the first 2 ac, only 1 ac confirmed a direct hit on the occupied site. 1 × 4 ship tasked with AI in the KTO. Good weather and photo coverage allowed the formation to acquire the target, an Arty Bty, early. The formation released 6 × MK 87 CBUs into the target area with 1 ac experiencing a hang up which he did not try and release in manual due to the close proximity of civilian housing. All ac encountered heavy AAA in the target area and the lead thought he saw a possible SAM 16 fired. 1 × 2 ship tasked with recce in the KTO. Due to failure of the F126 camera and the continuing difficulties with the LOROP the two targets were not covered.

**14 Feb**
1 × 4 ship tasked with AI in the KTO. The formation elected to use a higher dive angle against their target, an Arty Bty, with rewarding results. A total of 8 × MK 87 CBUs were released onto the target and all were confirmed to impact on Arty positions with some secondary explosions. On egress several of the flight experienced SA-2 lock up. 1 × 4 ship tasked with AI in the KTO. The formation had no problems acquiring their target, an Arty Bty, and using increased dive angle release parameters achieved some excellent results. BDA assessed visually and by HUD video as extensive damage done to the site with secondary explosions from the Command Post just behind the gun positions. Described by the lead as the most effective mission from his 4 ship to date. 1 × 4 ship tasked with AI in the KTO. In excellent weather the formation had no trouble in acquiring the target, a D20 Arty Bty, and released 8 × MK 87 CBUs. Due to the lack of ballistics 4 of them dropped slightly short of the DMPI but a successful mission all the same. 1 × 4 ship tasked with AI in the KTO. The target, a D20 Arty Bty, was achieved in excellent weather. Although the formation experienced some light AAA in the target area all × MK 87 CBUs were released. On egress two AAA sites were reported to the control agency for the A10s to play with. 1 × 2 ship tasked with recce in the KTO. Practice makes perfect as the saying goes. The pair achieved excellent coverage of both targets for the following day, an Arty Bty and Astros II MRL Bty, with both F126 and LOROP. This gives the pilots both high level imagery for target acquisition and detailed target coverage for selecting DMPIs.

## 15 Feb

1 × 4 ship tasked with AI in the KTO. Working with good imagery and in excellent weather the formation had little trouble finding their target, an MRL Bty. They released their 8 × MK87 CBUs onto the target while encountering AAA up to 12000ft. BDA was assessed by the following mission as severe damage done to the

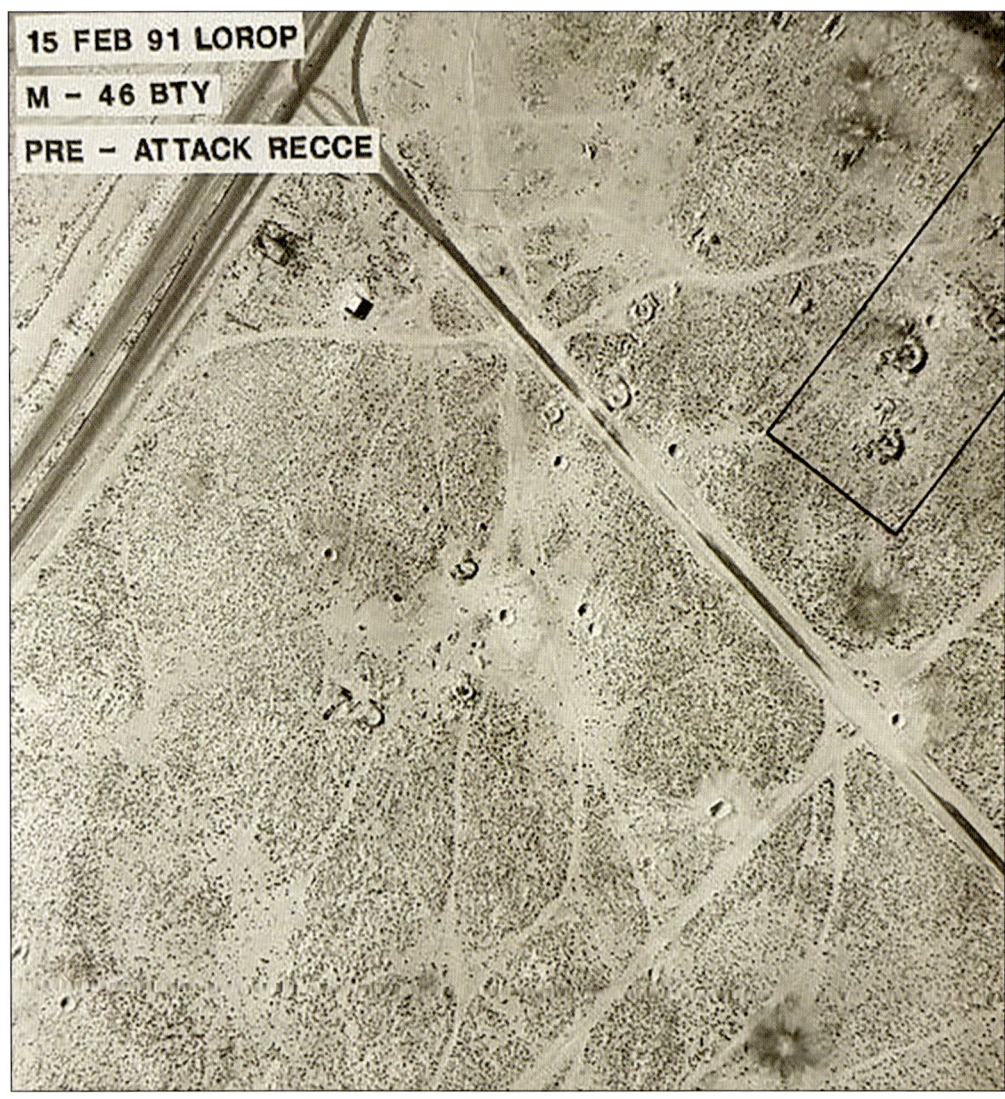

Imagery taken from the F126 LOROP camera on a mission conducted on 15 February prior to the attack on an Iraqi M46 Artillery position. It was flown by Squadron Leader Dave Bagshaw and Flight Lieutenant Pete Livesey, call sign Batsman 11. The LOROP camera was fitted to Flight Lieutenant Livesey's aircraft on this particular mission, Jaguar XZ358 'Diplomatic Service'. This target was later destroyed by eight MK 87 CBUs dropped by Jaguar aircraft. (*Courtesy W. Pixton*)

command and control facilities with several vehicles left burning. 1 × 4 ship tasked with AI in the KTO. The formation flew against the same MRL Bty as the above formation. Target acquisition was made difficult for the No 3 and 4 due to the arrival of 3 F16s releasing 12 bombs onto the same target. The formation managed to release their 8 × MK 87 CBUs onto the MRL Bty, and nearby artillery. 1 × 4 ship tasked with AI in the KTO. 1 ground abort. The formation found their target, a 2S1 Arty Bty, had already been decimated by a previous F18 mission and few, if any of the guns were touched. They released their 6 × Mk87 CBUs into the target area to mop up any stragglers. 1 × 4 ship tasked with AI in the KTO. Tasked against the same 2S1 Bty the formation found the fragged DMPI completely devastated and were able to shift to other suitable targets in what was a target rich environment. A total of 8 × Mk 87 CBUs were released on several Arty positions with good results confirmed visually with HUD film. 1 × 2 ship tasked with recce in the KTO. The pair flew the targets for the following day and produced good imagery on both F126 and LOROP cameras.

**16 Feb**
2 × 4 ship tasked with AI in the KTO. Both formations, tasked against artillery, found the whole of southern Kuwait hidden beneath a thick layer of black smoke, a result of the burning oil wells. Target acquisition was impossible, and the formation returned to base without releasing their weapons. 1 × 4 ship tasked with AI in the KTO. The formation found their target, an M46 Arty Bty, north of where the black smoke originated. Releasing 8 × Mk 87 CBUs onto several DMPIs, results were confirmed as good with several secondary explosions seen and several fires seen over the target area. The formation then went on to strafe an Army Barracks for good measure. On egress from Kuwait the formation experienced heavy AAA up to 15000ft. 1 × 4 ship tasked with AI in the KTO. The formation had few problems finding their target, an M46 Bty, in the clear area of Kuwait. Target tracking, however, was made difficult by heavy AAA in layers 8 – 10000ft, 15000ft and several explosions at higher levels. A total of 8 × MK87 CBUs were released onto the target but BDA was impossible as the formation were more interested in running away bravely from all the AAA.

**17 Feb**
4 × 4 ship tasked with AI in the KTO. All missions cancelled before getting airborne due to poor weather in the KTO. 1 × 2 ship tasked with recce in the KTO. Cancelled due to poor weather.

**18 Feb**
1 × 4 ship tasked with AI in the KTO. The formation found their primary target obscured by smoke so elected their alternate, a large logistics site. A total of

8 × MK87 CBUs were released onto several different revetted areas within the site. The formation encountered light AAA as they coasted out from Kuwait on return to base. 1 × 4 ship tasked with AI in the KTO. The extensive smoke in Kuwait made the formation release their 8 × MK 87 CBUs on their alternate target, the same logistics site as above. BDA was assessed as good with several secondary explosions see within the target area. 1 × 2 ship tasked with recce in the KTO. The smoke covering the majority of southern Kuwait pushed the pair further north to gain area coverage for the USMC. Results were good with several enemy positions found on the LOROP camera with accurate positions found on the F126. The pair managed BDA on the morning's target which confirmed that several revetted areas were on fire. 1 × 4 ship tasked with AI in the KTO. The formation elected to use a target, a logistics site, found by the recce pair. The site was extensive and 4 × 1000lb bombs and 4 × MK 87 CBUs were released with damage seen to be done to several revetted vehicles. 1 × 4 ship tasked with AI in the KTO. A very straight forward mission against the same logistics site. The formation found the target in clear air and released 4 × 1000lb bombs and 4 × MK 87 CBUs.

An artist's impression, similar to the morning combat mission that was flown on 18 February. A pair of Jaguar aircraft flying through the black smoke from the oil fields that were set ablaze by the retreating Iraqi army. (*Courtesy Roger Murray*)

## 19 February

1 × 4 ship tasked with AI in the KTO. The formation found their target, a 59-1 Arty Bty, in dense smoke. The target area was known to be an area of intense military activity, so the formation pressed home their attack picking individual revetted positions within the area. BDA was impossible due to the haze. One of the ac experienced SA-6 lockup in the target area. 1 × 4 ship tasked with AI in the KTO. While en route to the target area they were informed that the burning oil was obscuring their primary and alternate targets, both Arty positions. The formation were given new targets. Information from the controlling agency in an area of clear airspace and released their 8 × MK 87 CBUs onto Arty scrapes that they found. 1 × 4 ship tasked with AI in the KTO. The formation elected to go to their alternate target, an Arty Bty, when they realised that the smoke haze would be obscuring their primary target. All the 8 × Mk 87 CBUs were seen to impact on revetted areas but the thin smoke haze prevented them from confirming that the sites were occupied. 1 × 4 ship tasked with AI in the KTO. A straight forward mission going for their alternate target after an airborne weather update. The formation released 8 × MK 87 CBUs onto the Arty position, but BDA was difficult due to smoke haze. 1 × 2 ship tasked with recce in the KTO. The pair had several targets for planning purposes and BDA. While filming the pair encountered heavy AAA both at 12000ft, well above, and at 22000ft, not well below and managed to locate a 100mm AAA site as it fired. Having completed the target work the pair then did a complete sweep of the Kuwait/Saudi border area for the Army planners. Some excellent imagery obtained for both internal use and for the USMC and British Army.

## 20 Feb

1 × 4 ship tasked with AI in the KTO. The formation found their target in very poor weather and elected to go to their secondary target, a logistics site. The weather was again poor and No 3 did not acquire the target and returned with his weapons. The other 3 ac released 6 × MK 87 CBUs onto the site with visual confirmation of damage done to several SSVs. 1 × 4 ship tasked with ASI in the KTO. The primary target was obscured by cloud, so the formation released their 8 × MK 87 CBUs onto alternate target, an Arty Bty. Several DMPIs were chosen in what was known target rich environment. 1 × 4 ship tasked with AI in the KTO. 2 airborne aborts (1 escort). The remaining pair found their target, an MRL Bty, easily due to the excellent imagery provided by the recce pair. They released their 4 × MK 87 CBUs and saw possible secondary explosions. 1 × 4 ship tasked with AI in the KTO. The weather in the target area, an MRL Bty, but No 3 was unable to acquire the actual DMPI and did not release. The others released 6 × MK 87 CBUs onto revetted positions in the target area. 1 × 2 ship tasked with recce in the KTO and Iraq. The pair had a request to photograph 19 separate oil distribution points controlling the fire trenches along the

Squadron Leader Chris Allam taxing in a Jaguar, armed with CBU-87s. (*Courtesy C. Allam*)

Kuwait and Iraq border with Saudi Arabia, to confirm BDA from F117 attacks. The pair achieved 100% coverage of the points not obscured by cloud.

**21 Feb**
2 × 4 ships tasked with AI in the KTO. Both formations returned to base without releasing their weapon due to extensive cloud in the KTO. 1 × 4 ship tasked with AI in the KTO. The formation found their target, an MRL Bty, despite the black oil smoke, helped by good target imagery from a previous day. A total of 8 × MK 87 CBUs were released onto the target area with no secondary explosions seen, and BDA difficult because of the conditions. 1 × 4 ship tasked with AI KTO. The target an MRL Bty was difficult to identify through the oil smoke. The target area was an area of known enemy artillery concentration with accurate enemy positions confirmed by imagery. The formation released their 8 × MK 87 CBUs into the area were the MRL Bty was known to be but could not carry out BDA. 1 × 2 ship tasked with recce in the KTO. The pair had several targets to cover for both BDA and targeting requirements. This area was partially covered by oil smoke so having covered as much as possible elected to cover the open area of southern Kuwait and Kuwait/Saudi border defences for use by JFHQ in planning the ground offensive.

**22 Feb**
2 × 4 ships tasked with AI in the KTO. Both formations found that the target area was totally covered by smoke made worse by an inversion at 9,000ft. Communication

with USMC control agencies was difficult due to their short range equipment and use of secure comms that the Jaguar is incapable of using. Only one of the 4 ships achieved clearance, from a fast FAC, to release if they found a target. All ac returned to base without releasing their weapons. 1 × 4 ship tasked with AI in the KTO. The formation had been retasked with a target, a revetted Arty Bty, in the clear airspace further north of Kuwait. Target acquisition was easy for a change and 8 × MK 87 CBUs were released onto revetments. On egress from the target area the formation leader experienced an unguided SAM 2 in his 12 o'clock at short range. SOP tactics of running away bravely were employed and the formation returned to base unscathed. 1 × 4 ship tasked with AI in the KTO. The target, a revetted Arty Bty, was difficult to acquire in light haze. The first 2 ac dropped their 4 × MK 87 CBUs onto the prime DMPI and the second 2 ac released theirs onto an alternate Arty Bty nearby. BDA was assessed visually as good with secondary explosions seen at the primary target. The formation confirmed the necessity of good recce imagery to establish which Arty scrapes are occupied.

## 23 Feb

1 × 4 ship tasked with AI in the KTO. A move over to western Kuwait to target the Republican Guard made it necessary to AAR en route. The target, an Arty Bty, was found but was already being attacked by RSAF F5s. The formation flew to their alternate target area and released their 16 × 1000lb bombs onto a line of revetted Arty with secondary explosions seen along the line. A smooth mission with AAR and comms working well. 1 × 4 ship tasked with AI in the KTO. This was another mission against Republican Guard units. This formation had no problems with AAR and found that they were following 3 × B52s into the target area, an awesome sight as described by the formation leader. They found their primary target DMPI burning from a previous attack so released their 16 × 1000lb bombs onto an alternate Arty Bty. 1 × 4 ship tasked with AI in the KTO. In what was becoming the new Republican Guard target rich environment the formation found their target, an Arty Bty having AAA en route. The first 2 ac released 4 × MK 87 CBUs and the second ac released 4 × pods of CRV-7. BDA from the CRV-7, with the new software programme, was excellent with smoke seen to be coming from the Arty positions that were selected. 1 × 4 ship tasked with AI in the KTO. The formation refuelled and found their target in excellent weather. They released 8 × MK 87 CBUs onto V-shaped Arty positions in the target area. An eventful successful mission. 1 × 2 ship tasked with recce in Iraq. After AAR the pair transited to their target area over the mornings target for BDA. The target area was the destination of 1 BR Corps in the eventually of a ground war. The pair encountered lockup from SA-2, SA-6 and SA-8 while over the target but saw no mission. The imagery produced some excellent results with several occupied, revetted Republican Guard positions located.

**24 Feb**
1 × 4 ship tasked with AI in the KTO. The formation had problems finding their allotted tanker, due to very poor weather and ended up at 4,000ft. The lead aircraft experienced a burst of refuelling hose while on the basket and having fuel go down both engines and acrid blue smoke in the cockpit, returned to base. The rest continued with the refuel, on one hose, but the No 3 was outside his TOT bracket and also returned to base. The remaining 2 ac released their weapons onto their target, a Republican Guard Arty Bty, and saw secondary explosions as they pulled off. 1 × 4 ship tasked with AI in the KTO. The formation AAR in difficult conditions but found their target, a Republican Guard Arty Bty, in excellent weather. The frequency agile USMC control agencies ensured that clearance to release was not obtained until 2 minutes from their target. All 4 ac scored direct hits on their selected DMPIs with a total of 8 CRV-7 rocket pods. 1 × 4 ship tasked with AI in the KTO. The formation completed their AAR with no problems but having arrived in the target area were prevented from releasing due to the close proximity of friendly troops to their primary target, a Republican Guard Arty Bty. They were vectored onto more Arty further north and released their CRV-7 rocket pods to great effect. One of the formation saw possible IR missile fired at them in the target area. 1 × 4 ship tasked with AI in the KTO. 2 ac could not find the tanker, in rapidly deteriorating weather, and returned to base via a diversion to Al Jubail. The other 2 ac reached their target area but having passed through several control agencies, could not obtain clearance to release on their target, a Republican Guard Arty Bty, so returned to base. 1 × 2 ship tasked with recce in Iraq. The pair flew 2 large areas well into Iraq and encountered almost continual lockup from SA-2, SA-6 and SA-8. Some excellent imagery was obtained on the LOROP but due to a failure of the F126 it was unusable.

An RAF 55 Squadron Victor K2 tanker preparing to receive coalition aircraft for AAR. (*Courtesy RAFHB*).

**25 Feb**
4 × 4 ship tasked with AI in the KTO. All four formations managed to AAR but encountered bad weather over their target areas and returned to base without releasing any weapons. 1 × 2 ship tasked with recce in Iraq. The pair had no problem with AAR but having flown their target areas found extensive medium cloud cover which prevented any imagery being taken. The pair again encountered heavy SAM acquisition.

**26 Feb**
2 × 4 ship tasked with AI in the KTO. Both formations returned to base with their weapons due to extensive cloud cover in their target areas. 2 × 4 ships tasked with AI in the KTO. Both formations cancelled on the ground due to the poor weather. 1 × 2 ship tasked with recce in the KTO. The formation experienced the same poor weather as all the other formations had found but decided to have a look below it. They broke cloud at 1000ft and promptly had a SA-6 and SA-8 fired at them. Both missiles were successfully evaded, and the pair returned to base vowing never to fly recce again.

**27 Feb**
1 × 4 ship tasked with AI in the KTO. 1 × ground abort. The formation had no problems with AAR but when they arrived at their target area they were informed that

A Jaguar at Muharraq under a sun canopy loaded with a full weapon payload of 1,000lb GP bombs. (*Courtesy M. Cartwright*)

CSAR ops were on. The control agency vectored them to another Kill Zone, but poor weather precluded the release of any weapons. 1 × 4 ship tasked with AI in the KTO. The formation experienced severe problems with AAR due to bad weather conditions. Having completed the AAR, they found the same problem as the first formation with CSAR ops. All ac returned to base with weapons. 1 × 4 ship tasked with AI in the KTO. The formation arrived in the target area, having AAR, only to find poor weather and no clearances for release from the controlling agency. All ac returned to base with weapons. 1 × 2 ship tasked with recce in the Iraq. The pair flew the planned route, well into Iraq, but could not find any area with good enough weather to obtain imagery. 1 × 4 ship tasked with AI in the KTO. On arriving in the target area, having AAR, the formation were tasked to recce an alternate target by the USMC. The lead ac found a suitable target, but clearance was not obtained due to the close proximity of friendly forces. A very frustrating mission that turned out to be the last of the war.

## Training
The only training to take place during the month was some LGB work with the Buccaneers after their arrival from the UK. This was short-lived after it was decided that the Jaguars would continue with the weapons they had and the Tornado would be the LGB platform.

## Attachments and Detachments
There have been none during the period.

## Visits
A visit by the Joint Commander and AOC in C Strike Command Air Chief Marshal Sir Patrick Hine accompanied by COS HQBFME Air Commodore Ian McFadyen took place on the unit on 16/17 Feb.

## Social
During the period the war was being fought there were no specific social functions, however the luxury of living in a 5 star hotel did allow scope for relieving the tensions of the war missions. The war ended at 0500hrs GMT on 27 Feb 91, to coincide with the 54th birthday of Sqn Ldr Dave Bagshaw. As expected the relief of all those involved in the war took the form of a rather large, spontaneous party which moved from location to location before finally coming to rest in OC Jag Det's modest little hotel suite. Although not the end of the war it was the cessation of hostilities until a peace agreement could be worked out between all the interested parties, and good enough excuse for a party. There were no speeches and few toasts, the pilots preferring to enjoy their own company in the thought that they did not have to get shot at again.

Operations Record Book January–February 1991 (RAF 540)  43

An impressive photo of the nose of a Jaguar with its distinctive chisel nose. (*Courtesy 41 Sqn, RAF*)

The reverse of a Jaguar aircraft standing in the intense heat, displaying its powerful Mk104 engines. (*Courtesy 41 Sqn ORB, RAF*)

# Chapter 4

# Pilots' Personal Extracts

An informal photograph taken of all pilots on Jaguar XZ364 'Saddam'. (*Courtesy M. Rainier*)

The squadron diary reads, 'The Strike Gang in a macho pose', L–R: Flying Officer Mal Rainier, Squadron Leader Mike Gordon, Flight Lieutenants Steve Thomas and Roger Crowder. (*Courtesy 41 Sqn ground crew*)

'Team tab, before hitting the "Londoner"'(a bar near the Diplomat), L–R: Wing Commander Bill Pixton, Flight Lieutenants Pete Tholen, Ted Stringer and Flying Officer Nick Collins standing in front of Jaguar XX725 'Johnny Fartpants'. (*Courtesy P. Tholen*)

'The mid 5-ship', named after Dick Midwinter, L–R: Flight Lieutenants Toby Craig, Simon Young, Squadron Leader Midwinter with mascot Ed the Duck, and Flight Lieutenant Dick MacCormac. (*Courtesy S. Young*)

## Squadron Leader Chris Allam

Chris was designated as executive officer (XO) for the Jaguar roulemont:

> I was with Baggers, Shutty, Nick Collins, and Craig Hill. We were out in Texas when Saddam invaded Kuwait. We saw it all unfolding on a big screen in a bar in the hotel. We were all pretty pissed off, though even being in Texas, we wanted to be there. We rang Pixton up and said get us back. Him turning around and saying, 'Don't worry you will get your chance.' I remember, we were meant to be working with Victor tankers. Getting into work one morning and scribbled on a board was written 'Victors have gone home!'

Keen to follow developments, Chris received the latest information from members of the Jaguar force already deployed on operations. However, in the days before the internet and modern forms of communication a telephone call was the best he could achieve:

> We got phone calls from guys out there. They said, if Saddam continued or certainly came into Saudi, we had a mission, somewhere in Kuwait where we would launch all twelve aircraft against a specific pre-determined target. Going in at low level and pull up at a 20 degree and dive bomb. I think the French actually did this at the start of the operation and got shot to hell. I am glad we did not do that!

Chris, being the Exec, was nominated in the first rotation of four pilots to deploy to Bahrain:

> It was me, Craig Hill, Steve Shutt, and Roger Crowder, leaving the UK on 5 November. I remember that as when we took off from RAF Brize Norton it was firework night. We flew to Saudi, and a Herc took us around and, bizarre, it was the only time a Herc captain shook my hand when I got off the aircraft. We arrived got drunk, as you normally do on the first night, then started work the following day.

After two weeks the handover was complete, and Chris spoke to Wing Commander Bill Pixton with his thoughts:

> I said, 'I think this how we should operate, not tactical, but how a squadron operate in the UK.' We did not need to fly 16,000 hours a day and seven days week, there was no need. We, Tornados and the French Jaguars were the only aircraft planning low level. There was a change about two weeks before we started to fly at medium level, higher if we can.
>
> We learnt how demanding flying over the desert is at extremely low levels and brushed up on our air-to-air refuelling skills.

L–R: In the operations planning room, Squadron Leaders Mike Gordon, Chris Allam and an unknown wing commander (back facing). Reading a bluey from home is Flight Lieutenant Stevie Thomas. (*Courtesy M. Gordon*)

Chris remembers well the morning of 17 January when waking up at 2 a.m. in his room at the Diplomat Hotel:

> We had all been briefed on the ATO some days before the deadline expired. Even so I was surprised when I was woken on the morning of 17 January to the sound of Tornados getting airborne on their first mission. I switched on the television to watch CNN. Already it seemed, judging by the news reports, that Iraq was on fire: surely no nation could survive this massive onslaught! The night raids had their desired effect and Saddam Hussein would soon be surrounded. Relief; I would not be needed to fly. However once at work, more realism took over.

The morning of 17 January, Chris was on ground alert, as flight commander of a four-ship, call sign Keeper 85, comprising of Flight Lieutenants Craig Hill, Steve Shutt, and Dave Foote:

> It was just like a tactical evaluation, I thought. I sat listening to the electronic warfare officers, intelligence officers and GLOs briefs. With the other members of my constituted four, I went through the air tasking order message, which had details of our mission. We were on standby on thirty-minute ground alert for close air support. We planned and briefed the mission, went to the aircraft, and put them on state and then returned to the squadron operations room to wait the message to go. We were all immensely relieved when the first Tornado mission arrived safely back at Bahrain. Hopefully, our mission would go equally as well. After about six hours on ground alert my mission was stood down, the tension was lifted, jokes were told, and we were soon on our way back to the hotel.

*Left*: Squadron Leader Chris Allam. (*Courtesy M. Gordon*)

*Below*: Preparing for a combat mission, climbing into Jaguar XZ119 'Katrina Jane'. (*Courtesy A. Emtage*)

On 19 January Chris was flight commander of a four-ship, call sign Longstop 02, flying Jaguar XZ118 'Buster Gonad'. The flight comprised Flight Lieutenants Craig Hill, Steve Shutt, and Dave Foote and took off at 0855:

> We were on thirty-minute alert for CAS. We did not expect to be launched. Then from our tasking authority in Riyadh a flash message. A mission for us to Iraq, time over target two hours. Mayhem. Maps were found, thoughts were gathered, then the automatic routine took over. We were ready to go, final brief from the GLO, people wished us luck, we in turn tried to smile, not really showing how we felt. The

Al fresco lunch at the back of the Ops block, L-R Flight Lieutenants Steve Shutt, Dave Foote, Squadron Leader Chris Allam, and Flight Lieutenant Craig Hill. (*Courtsey of C. Allam*)

engineers had prepared the aircraft. More good wishes. A final walk around the jet, all the pins were out. A final nervous chat with the ground crews helping me to strap in, then a smile and he was gone, and I was on my own. I went through the mission in my mind, reminding myself of the lessons the pilots learnt the day before and telling myself that I wouldn't make the same mistakes. Almost before I was ready it was time to start engines: no problems there, as usual the Jaguar was fully serviceable. Check-in time arrived; everyone was on frequency, serviceable and ready to go.

Once airborne I carried out operational checks to make sure all the aircraft systems were working. The electronic countermeasures pod self-tested, lighting up the rear warning radar.

Checking in with the AWACs, Longstop flight were given 'picture clean' from the AWACs controller, no Iraqi aircraft airborne. They continued on their mission and headed north towards their target in Iraq. On being handed over to a ground call sign, they were informed the weather was poor in the target area and a secondary target was selected in Kuwait:

The weather improved as we crossed the border. ECM pod was in automatic mode, weapon switches were made live and the RWR started to light up, indicating all manner of systems, some friendly, some not. I took in some of this information, then the target area was approaching. Weapon aiming selected, find the target and into the dive for an eternity, in reality only seconds, and then the weapons were released, and I started to climb away. No time for battle damage assessment, but my bombs appeared to have exploded in the area of the target. We actually did not see the target and we dropped through the cloud. Back over the Gulf I had time to think clearly. I checked in the rest of the formation, they were all there, weapons delivered. In no time at all we were taxiing in at Bahrain. Smiles, handshakes, and congratulations all round, nobody was thinking that we might have to do this again tomorrow. Back to the squadron operations room. Debrief the mission with the GLO, EWO and IO and then back to the hotel for the squadron nightly debrief. When I got back we got a bollocking for dropping through the cloud. 'Try and not drop bombs unless you can see the target.' I will try and remember that next time. So ended my first day of operational flying.

The sortie landing back at Bahrain at 1005:

You only saw your four-ship, the GLO and the engineers. Life was pretty insular really.
  We were always left to own devices, we weren't the glamour boys, we weren't the Harrier, we weren't the Tornado, we were the Jaguar and just get on with it. AVM Bill Wratten was not too happy with us flying at 20ft. The boss turning around and saying what do you want us to do, what are you going to do about it? We want to practise for war, and it all went away. My final thoughts are best summarised in the words spoken by one of the guys, 'It's the first time I have ever seen tracer coming up at me. It was the longest minute of my life, I can tell you.'

Squadron Leader Chris Allam standing beside Jaguar XZ106 'Rule Britannia' at RAF Akrotiri en route to the UK on the 'leopard trail' on completion of combat operations. (*Courtesy C. Allam*)

## Squadron Leader David (Baggers) Bagshaw

Dave was the RAF representative of the detachment commander of the Jaguar force at RAM 90 at Bergstrom air force base, Texas, in July 1990:

> We were billeted downtown, I got up one morning and turned on the TV to CNN, low and behold there were Jaguars taxiing by. This was the first inkling of the first deployment to the Gulf. The rest of the team came running in and said had I seen this. 'We don't want to keep this competition going, we want to join these guys.' I had to tell them to not be mutinous about this, we are here to do the competition.

Returning to RAF Coltishall, Dave, or Baggers as he was more commonly known, paid careful attention to the operations that his colleagues were conducting in Oman.

He deployed early as part of the second roulement, arriving at Bahrain on a C-130 at 3 am on 27 November 1990 with fellow pilot Dave Foote and Engineering Warrant Officer Mick Cartwright:

> As we had been doing for decades, ultra-low level wherever we could, thinking fast and low option, that's what we did when we got out to Saudi.

Squadron Leader Dave Bagshaw flying Jaguar XX725 'Johnny Fartpants' on a mission over Kuwait. (*Courtesy 41 Sqn, RAF*)

Going down the mini Gulf and wiz around low level. You would be sitting there, alternating doing the 'duty bounce', for whatever four-ship was operating, and you could see this wave come for miles and this was our aircraft. In fact, Stevie Thomas displayed a sand wake as well as the water variety!

Word came trickling down from Riyadh that our main focus was going to be artillery targets, the army were really concerned about chemical or biology artillery heading their way before they headed across the border. I missed out on the first ten days because I was expecting delivery of a new set of eyeglasses. I consulted the boss, stating that due to the potential threat of the Iraqi air defence system, I was uncertain of my ability to warn my wingy of a MIG in his 6 o'clock or a SAM inbound.

Dave acted as operations officer until his new glasses arrived and got stuck into helping out his fellow pilots with planning and scheduling missions:

When my new specs arrived, they were no bloody good either! I went back to the boss to discuss my future employment. After a fortnight as Ops Officer sitting in on mission debriefs, it became apparent that the Iraqi Air to Air and SAM threat had been largely negated by Coalition forward fighter CAPs and the EW guys, the USAF Weasels and USN EA-6Bs with their effective jamming and Anti-Radar Missiles.

Wing Commander Pixton considered the option of my getting back to operational flying and recommended that I join his formation. I leapt at this chance and flew my first combat mission on 29 January flying XZ106 'Rule Britannia' with callsign Batsman mission carrying the LOROP operationally for the first time.

It is reported in the comments on the authorisation sheets that AAA puffs were observed:

We would go for known and sometimes unknown targets. We were spotting places like gun emplacements that were not being tasked. We would come and tell Tom, our guy in Riyadh, and say: 'Did you know about this one.' That would come up as our target the next day.

Flight Lieutenant Pete Livesey and Dave would form part of a formation and would break away as a recce pair and collect intelligence of targets and provide detailed photographic information for HQ to help with future missions.

Though having a primary role to conduct recce missions, Dave still carried out many combat engagements of targets and recalls:

Getting to grips with dive bombing profile was a steep learning curve. The climb was continuous to the IP using part throttle reheat as required to maintain a decent rate of climb. The target was usually acquired before the IP, climbing until the tip in point, aiming to achieve max altitude to ensure a 60 deg dive for optimum

*Above and below*: Squadron Leader Dave Bagshaw preparing for a mission. (*Courtesy D. Bagshaw and A. Emtage*)

accuracy with our dumb bombs. I recall seeing 34,000 ft in the HUD when commencing the necessarily gentle wingover to enter the dive. It was essential to throttle back immediately to avoid exceeding the optimum 450K, track the target and commit to release the bombs to enable dive recovery above 15,000 ft.

During my baptism of steep dive bombing and exposure to unfriendly fire, the powers that be decided that the Desert Cats' reconnaissance assets should be usefully tasked with providing Bomb Damage Assessment and battlefield Areas of Interest imagery. As such, Flight Lieutenant Pete Livesey and myself were assigned to operate the aircraft fitted with (1) the LOROP and (2) the conventional recce pod mounting the F126 survey and F95 low oblique cameras. Mission results would hopefully assist headquarters planners with relatively up to date intelligence. The pair would be 'grafted on' to a Desert Cat attack formation for the ingress phase, then peel off to go about their tasked business. These sorties were usually flown at 25,000ft, from which the F126 camera coincidentally produced imagery of the scale 1:50,000 (very useful for target planning) and the LOROP gave remarkably clear cover of the same area but with much better target detail. Initially, excellent weather prevailed, but latterly, after Saddam had ordered the oilfields set alight, the ensuing pall of oily black smoke increasingly curtailed the success of both attack and recce missions during the final week and a half of hostilities. Such was the case of the Recce Pair's final mission. Livo and I had been tasked to cover an area north of Kuwait International; as we left the ops room, one of the PIs asked, 'Hey, if you're anywhere near Kuwait City, can you have a look and see if the water towers are still intact?' There was concern that they might have been destroyed, creating problems for the remaining inhabitants as well as the advancing liberators. I said we'd have a go on the way back – I think Livo said something like 'You're off your trolley!' Anyhow, we duly found that the smoke prevented any sight of the target area. Our return route did take us near Kuwait City, and as it appeared on the Projected Map Display, I called Livo saying 'I guess I'll have a stab at it.' Wishing to have no part of this madness, he pressed on home alone. As no hostile threats appeared on the HUD or pinged on the RWR, I set off down through the oily acrid cloud. I broke out at a comfortable 2000ft, looked right, and sho' nuff, there they were, still visually intact. With only vertically orientated cameras, I rolled 90 left to bring them to bear, took the shot and climbed back up through the murk and continued on home.

Dave was one of the most experienced front-line pilots on the Jaguar force and a historic moment that was recorded while on operations was the completion of 4,000 hours on this specific type of combat aircraft:

Ah yes, the 4,000 hours sortie and aftermath. The date was 8 January, a pair, me in XX962, Fat Slags, and the boss. It was an exercise, Fish Barrel, simulated

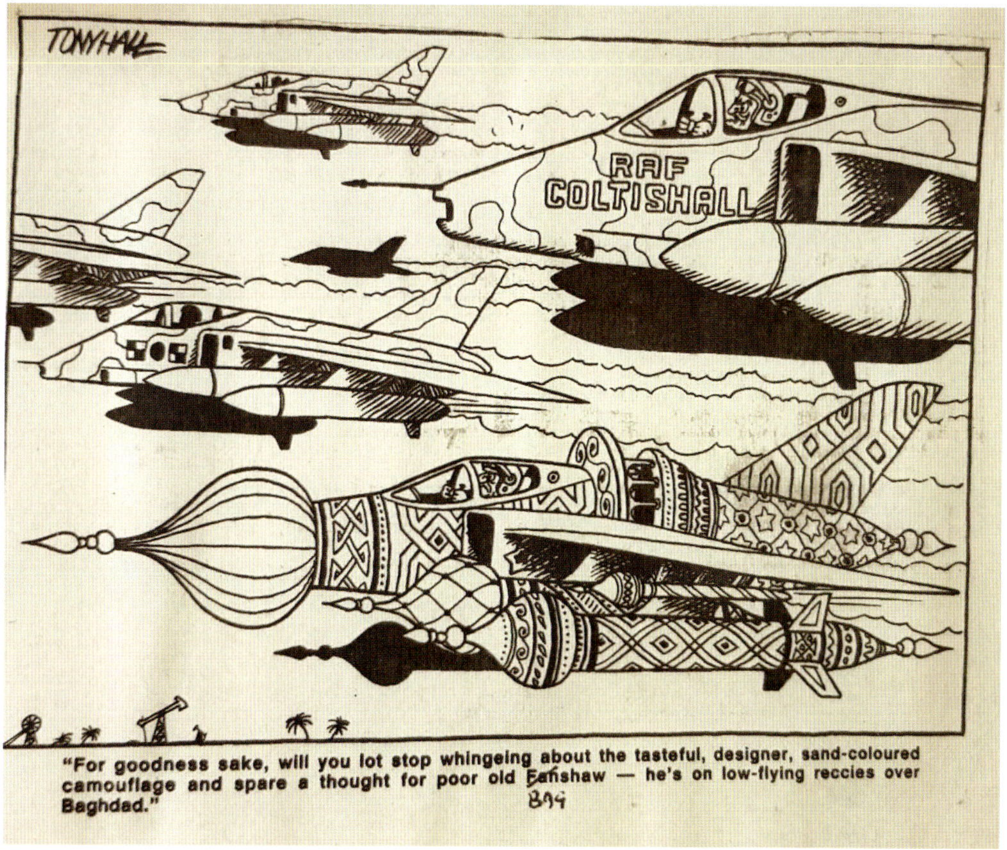

## Pilots' Personal Extracts

"For goodness sake, will you lot stop whingeing about the tasteful, designer, sand-coloured camouflage and spare a thought for poor old Fanshaw — he's on low-flying reccies over Baghdad."

A cartoon drawing taken from a UK newspaper, note the surname change to Bagshaw. (*Courtesy D. Bagshaw*)

Squadron Leader Dave Bagshaw standing in front of his aircraft, Jaguar XX733 'Pink Spitfire', with Jaguar XZ358 'Diplomatic Service' in the background. They have just landed at RAF Akrotiri on the 'leopard trail' on the return journey to the UK at the end of hostilities. (*Courtesy D. Bagshaw*)

*Above, left and opposite*: A series of photos taken on completion of a sortie on 8 January and the welcome celebration from the remaining pilots, flying Jaguar XX962 'Fat Slags'. It is recorded in the operational diary as, 'Baggers passes yet another milestone in Jaguar history. Baggers is the No 1 of the worldwide Jaguar pilots, and possibly the only one whoever will fly 4000hrs on the jet.' (*Courtesy 41 Sqn, RAF*)

Pilots' Personal Extracts 57

30-degree free fall and Level High Velocity Aircraft Rocket on a range north of Dhahran. RTB and taxi back to revetments to be greeted with 4,000 hours placard, and chaps and bubbly. To be honest, although it was never gonna be a 'non-event', I don't have a detailed recollection of the ensuing festivities, other than the usual intake of suitable beverages in the Diplomat Penthouse Bar and later downstairs being entertained by the resident Filipino/Filipina rock band. I must have recovered reasonably well, as I flew a two-hour, twenty-minute sortie the following day as No. 3 of eight Jags, which were part of a pre-hostility package mission including USAF F-4G Wild Weasels and USMC F-18s. AAR from a Victor, then ultra-low level in Saudi LFAs. This was the last but one sortie before the 'balloon went up'.

## Flight Lieutenant Toby Craig

Toby initially deployed to Thumrait, Oman, with 6 Squadron in early August 1990 when the Gulf War conflict broke out. He remembers the Jaguar aircraft being painted desert pink and a team of pilots were selected:

Dick MacCormac and I were on 6 squadron, and the most junior of the guys that went, with Mal Rainier. I went out in a VC10 to Thumrait, we then spent several months expecting war to kick off tomorrow. We planned to operate out of Thumrait with tanker support. And we thought the whole operation would be flown at low level, everything we trained for was at low level. The gloves were off in regard to restriction to altitude, we flew around the Oman desert at very low altitude. We flew almost every day, ultra-low level attacking simulated targets on the ground.

One of the issues flying solo you think you are invisible; you are below the radar coverage but if you are a visual capping fighter the size of your aircraft is matched by your shadow, which is a black Jaguar. It's exactly the same size of your aircraft the lower you are. Some sorties, if I were the bounce aircraft doing the attack playing the air defender, you would just have to look and you would see the black Jaguar flying around, you could not see the aeroplane, but you could see the shadows. They were quite easy to find so the best altitude was a bit higher where your shadow disappeared, and you only ducked down if you needed to, if you were either attacked by another air-air fighter or there was an area of SAMs. We could simulate that we could locate a physical location on the map, but we did not have any emitters that could simulate actual electronic warfare and get the indications that we would get in the cockpit that would show threats. We would be flying around and say, 'SAM 8, right, 2 o'clock', and then react to it, going through the motions of putting out chaff, flares or whatever the appropriate action was to that missile system. Runaway bravely, as that was what the Jaguar was best at! What we were really trying to do was progress to the target and evade the threat.

A photograph taken by Flight Lieutenant Toby Craig of Flight Lieutenant Dick MacCormac in October 1990 flying OLF over the desert returning to Thumrait. He recalls: 'A lot of the training was being conducted in Oman, through the UAE. High-level transit, low-level sortie and high level back.' (*Courtesy T. Craig*)

Flight Lieutenant Toby Craig on 10 October 1990 preparing to fly an unknown Jaguar from Thumrait to Bahrain. (*Courtesy T. Craig*)

On completion of his operational tour, Toby was posted back to the UK and arrived back at RAF Coltishall in November 1990:

> In November I was posted back to the UK when we did the full roulement thing. The whole team changed. Back in the UK we maintained currency. Effectively there was a four-ship on standby every week to ten days to go out the door with their bags packed. I got a phone call on mobile to say, 'You are off tomorrow.' I was playing golf at the time, so stopped that and went back to tell the wife I was off to the war! We joined the gang. We had already done the medium-level training, so we were already accomplished at that skill set. It was just getting used to operating in a new team. It was about 21 January 1991 that we were back in Bahrain.

On 24 January Toby flew on his second combat mission of the war, piloting Jaguar XZ358 'Diplomatic Service' as No. 3 in Keeper flight. The target was an Iraqi M46 artillery position:

> Dick and I were on a sortie and a pair, flew up together. Dick dived in on the target and dropped four 952 fused weapons. He pulled off, and I tipped in behind him. I saw an explosion in front on me, initially I thought this was AAA. I did not think it was his aircraft because it was like a black smoke explosion rather than an aeroplane exploding so I knew Dick had not been hit by an air-to-air missile. He pulled off, I carried on my attack because I did not think it was a threat to me and I was slightly off his axis. It was in my HUD, afterwards when we landed and I could see this thing going off and it turned out it was a 952 fuse 1,000lb going off about 10,000ft. He had cleared luckily; we had a safety manoeuvre after you release. But that specific weapon fused on arming.

Precision weaponeering was in its infancy during the Gulf War and Toby describes how he would release retard weapons onto a target:

> Pete Tholen and Stevie Thomas, our QWIs looking at some of the threats around Kuwait City, soon realised they were heavily defended by SA-6 and SA-8, so a decision was made to turn our training from low-level to high-level delivery. It is not a comfortable space for the Jaguar! It's underpowered, a decent weapon-aiming system, but it did not take into effect wind. There were lots of issues when dropping unguided weapons, 15,000ft–20,000ft and being accurate enough, so we did some modifications on our algorithms of the ballistics of the weapons, so they became more accurate and we practised our profiles at high-level dive. It is not as easy as it sounds. When you are getting an automated release you need an automated rather than manual release to get an accurate

Written in the squadron diary, 'Jake and Elwood pose before going sausage side.' L–R: Flight Lieutenants Toby Craig and Dick MacCormac standing in front of Jaguar XZ364 'Saddam'. They were nicknamed the Blues Brothers and always wore shades and had badges on their flight suits that read, 'We are on a mission from god'. (*Courtesy S. Young*)

weapons delivery. We released our weapons anything from 10,000ft–20,000ft. Average, 12,000ft–15,000ft. You spotted your weapons, there was your instant battle damage assessment. You looked for your target and saw how close your weapons went to the target. It was not like modern GPS-guided weapons where you expected to hit the target. This was all up to you, some skill and some luck. Because we would drop a stick of four weapons, if you target was quite small you would hope somewhere between your first and second, third, fourth bomb was your target! Sometimes they would be long and sometimes they would be short. Mostly there was a straddle, it was very difficult to assess what you damaged.

Ninety-five per cent of our targets were well away from any civilian buildings. I remember one target, a Silkworm site on the coast of Kuwait. We attacked that target between us a dozen times, thinking it was a threat to shipping, being a surface-surface missile, because we could not get battle damage assessment to say it was destroyed. If you take a picture of a Silkworm site from 20,000ft you can't tell if it has got holes in it. You can tell if it has fallen over. I am convinced we made this target inoperative very early on, but we kept going back against it.

Toby recalled Jaguar tactics and how these helped him not to be shot down in combat, and how he had a lucky escape on one mission:

We planned as an eight-ship, sometimes four-ships, what happened in practice was because we wanted to be random and erratic in our formation attacks and timings. Even if we were attacking the same target we did not want to repeat, say in two minutes another Jaguar would be coming over the target. We would organise our pairs so we would be moving around in different directions. The pair ahead could be ten minutes ahead, not the standard two minutes, so we would be unpredictable.

One sortie I remember, it was the closest to being shot down. We always aimed above the flak belt, the altitude the flak burst at was 10,000ft–12,000ft. We aimed to drop our weapons and have time to recover back above the flak belt. You had to make sure you tipped in with enough time to release your weapon with your given dive angle, and still be able to pull out. I tipped in too early and set up my dive path. It meant my approach angle was wrong, it meant the automated weapon release did not happen at 8,000ft, so I found myself a bit lower than I wanted to be. At about 12,000ft I started to see flashes around my cockpit, when I realised I was just flying through the flak and back out the other side. I dropped my weapon, and it was all OK. However, I could see it out the corner of my eye. On the recovery, on releasing your weapon we had a manoeuvre to get yourself out of the envelope of the weapon detonating prematurely, so if the 952 fuse went off early we planned for that.

On 23 January, during Toby's first mission, a USAF F-16 from the 614th Tactical Fighter Squadron, call sign Wolf 01, crashed and its pilot had to bail out into the Persian Gulf:

We heard it all on the radio. We heard the US pilot coming up saying his wingman had ejected and looking for parachutes. This then changed to a CSAR frequency. Those sort of things bring it home to you, every time you put yourself in that position you are vulnerable. You are just a human being, we are not immortal.

The following statement is taken from *Combat Search and Rescue in Desert Storm*, published by Air University, and relevant to this particular air accident:

The flight were attacking an interdiction target near Kuwait City. Immediately after it dropped its bombs, the aircraft burst into flames. The pilot, Major Jon Ball, was able to glide out over the Persian Gulf before ejecting. The orbiting AWACS monitored his Mayday call and notified the JRCC, who tasked the mission to the US Navy. The Navy RCC launched an SH-60, call sign Spade 50, from HSL-44. It was stationed aboard the USS *Nicholas*, on combat recovery duty in the northern Gulf area. Two USMC AV-8s were diverted to provide escort. Locating the survivor, the helicopter dropped two SEALs who rescued the pilot. Returning to their base, the pilots in Wolf flight reviewed the mission to determine what shot down Wolf 01. None of the other flight members could recall any active SAM indications or AAA airbursts or tracers. One of the flight members had happened to turn on his HUD recording device and had filmed Wolf 01 releasing his bombs. The film clearly showed one of its MK 84 2,000-pound bombs detonating just under the aircraft. The fragmentation pattern from the bomb enveloped the aircraft and brought it down. On that mission, the MK 84 bombs were loaded with special electronic FMU-139 fuses. In investigating the incident, the squadron determined that an 'anomaly' had been discovered in the operational testing by the producer of the fuse, Motorola, but any mention of this problem had been excluded. The 614th TFS did not use any more FMU-139 fuses in Desert Storm.

It is interesting to note that the Jaguar force were not the only aircraft type to suffer from premature weapon fusing.

For the pilots, having time off and being accommodated in a luxurious hotel, the Diplomat, it was a strange feeling to be conducting high-intensity combat one moment and then relaxing in a peacetime setting of a hotel:

It was very bizarre to go and drop a weapon in a serious war, and we could be at the end of that day, lying by the swimming pool at the Diplomat ordering a club sandwich, which was the food of choice! There were a lot of good restaurants around. Copper Chimney was a favourite curry house we went to. Upper Tree, cuppa tea, a fantastic place!

The Diplomat Hotel, where the Jaguar force were accommodated once they had moved to Bahrain. (*Author's collection*)

Flight Lieutenants Dick MacCormac and Toby Craig posing with 'Ed the Duck'. This photo appeared in the *London Evening Standard* on 31 January 1991. (*Courtesy T. Craig*)

Another event that Toby recalls with humour:

> The media was always outside. We had an 'Ed the Duck', it was somebody's puppet, I don't recall whose. And it flew many of its sorties in either Dick's or my cockpit. We would take it flying and one time we were met when we got out of the aeroplane and did this random pose, and the picture appeared in *London Evening Standard*. We got signed copies of the photo from Ed the Duck, it all became a bit of a joke.
>
> I must tell you about Dick and Craig's TV take-offs! We would take off as a pair, stay at low level. We would separate as we egressed away with flares. We would then pull up to 20 degrees with a fully armed aircraft. Do an aileron roll, and then in battle formation climb away, we would test the guns as soon as we got over the sea. It was absolute madness thinking about it now. There was a fully unstable Jaguar and we used to do these TV take-offs.

Toby reflected on his service in the Jaguar force and his thoughts on the conflict:

> Being a Jaguar pilot, we worked hard, played hard. The Jaguar force was genuinely very professional in what we did, with similar-minded people and decent chaps.
>
> I remember getting met by media after one sortie. They interviewed me, it was my second or third sortie, and I said to them, 'It was a successful mission, however I am glad I am not in the Army. We drop weapons from 15,000ft and we see them explode but we don't see the impact of these bombs. The Army fight their way through all this, all the time.' It was the nasty human element; we became detached from the physical impact on the humanity.

*Above and below*: Jaguars conducting a non-standard, TV take-off. (*Courtesy D. Bagshaw*)

Flight Lieutenant Toby Craig seated in the cockpit of Jaguar XZ364 'Saddam'. (*Courtesy T. Craig*)

## Flight Lieutenant Alex (E.T.) Emtage

'Why E.T? A pretty boring story really. When I arrived at 41 Squadron during September '88, I didn't have a personal call sign. This was mainly to be used on the programme board to show formation constitutions etc. but was often used in the air. The norm was to use the first three letters of the surname. The senior junta decided that EMT was awkward in the air, and as I was not the best of lookers it was decided to drop the M, therefore becoming ET. It stuck and I carried it through all my subsequent postings and still sometimes get called it today.

Alex was serving with 41 Squadron at the time of the Gulf War, knowing the roulemont was going to occur:

We were training, some intensive, doing what we had always done, which was the low-level work. Knowing a month before and the squadron moving en masse. Travelling down to RAF Brize Norton. The only thing that was noticeable, Helen, my wife was driving me there. When we got through the gate the news came that Keith Collister had been killed during low level training over the desert. I can remember looking at her face and it had completely dropped!

Arriving at Bahrain, one of Alex's first duties was to be part of a burial party to repatriate Flight Lieutenant Collister:

My first duty was pole bearer, there was six of us that put him on the back of a Herc. I remember how heavy it was because it was lead lined.

Not having long to reflect on his friend and colleague, it was straight into preparing for combat operations and reflecting on the type of training that was conducted:

Early on myself and Hoppy were teamed up as he seconded to 41 from 6, so we were very familiar with each other's style by the time we deployed. As low level was expected, OLF was routine and we became very comfortable at 100ft. It also became clear that the 100ft that we were comfortable with was too high, as I found out when I flew my famil [familiar] formation when my lead was 'well' below me … And I mean well below. After Keith's crash, the Det lost the 50ft MSD auth, although the DetCo just said, 'Do what is required to be ready.' Initially ultra-low was hard work, but in time I was comfortable operating at 20–30ft while maintaining lookout etc, etc … then we went in at medium level! That said, we practised with lots of weapons, even got to drop a couple of BL755s. I think there must have been a two-week transition period, and that period there was the first

The wreckage of Flight Lieutenant Keith Collister's aircraft, from 54 Squadron. He was killed on 13 November 1990 flying Jaguar GR1 XX754 at low level over the Qatari desert, 100 miles south of Bahrain, when he hit a hidden sand ridge. Cleared to 50ft, he clipped the top of the ridge, which was at an exact height of 87ft. Wing Commander Jerry Connolly attended the Air Investigation Branch findings. He flew an aircraft on the same heading on the same flight path. The only reason that he saw the ridge was that people were standing on top of it. (*Courtesy Desertstorm.com*)

> alert was pulled as the Iraqis started their Scud attacks. We all got woken up and in NBC conditions when the Scud were going to land.
>
> We had a pre-op brief, which we were given by an intelligence officer, briefing everyone, 'You are going to do that and you this.' He looked at the Jaguar guys and said, 'I wouldn't want to do your job, you are doing close air support in Kuwait theatre of operations.' We all went 'What!' He really made real fun of it, the fact we were doing it daytime, inside a defended area! The most important brief of your life and he is was making fun of it all!

Flying in combat, tactics were changed to suit the type of missions that were being executed. Alex recalls why it was so important not to set a pattern in the sky and how surface-to-air threats were a constant threat:

> The SEAD boys did a grand job! We very quickly went from eight balls, to four balls, to pairs. We found on an attack that the first pair inevitably got away

unscarred. When the first bombs went in you got barraged by AAA. It was not heavy, but it was just like the Second World War. On our first attack we came out below the clouds, so it was fairly dark underneath. That time there was a few more guns around and the whole area was just twinkling. Having one close call, on a speed boat target, I was entering the dive. We had already done a CRV-7 attack. While you have no dramas going down, the Jaguar suffers on the recovery. You then get back into the circle looking down and going in to open up with guns. As I tipped in, all I can remember is a glowing dart going past my cockpit window. I also saw an SA-2 being ballistically fired. Straight line, straight up. It caught my attention; this thing goes like stink! If I hadn't seen it, you would have a warning, this thing coming up to get your eyes on. I don't think you could have avoided it; it was going that quick! It was about a mile and half from me.

You could see the bombs hit, as you were recovering, about thirty seconds later you looked down. I cannot remember one of mine not going off.

On 19 January Alex was flying Jaguar XZ106 'Rule Britannia' as part of call sign Keeper flight:

We would fly in kill zones. I cannot remember where this particular kill box was, but we tipped in on the coordinates we had been given and there was nothing there. Hoppy and I were flying as the last pair of 8 aircraft and as I was pulling out of the dive, I saw four 1,000-pounders hitting about 3 miles ahead. I went there at 10,000ft just below the cloud(!) and saw the distinctive shape of an SA-2 site before entering the dive to deliver my weapons.

Alex recalls taking off with humour. With the laden weight of an array of weapons on board the Jaguar, it would need a long runway:

Take-offs could be interesting. As you began to run out of runway you'd start to pull back and you were just clearing the main road, by not a lot with four 1,000-pounders on board and ECM and two winders. Until you got to flying speed you were struggling a bit. That said you were getting people tipping in at 35,000ft. You were on the Alpha warning much of the time! People later asked 'How did you enter the dive?' Just let go of the stick and the aircraft does it for you. The problem was the recovery, as you just bleed all the energy. That is where it lacked performance. If we had to do any real dodging, to get away from bad stuff, it could be a struggle.

*Above and below*: Flight Lieutenant Alex Emtage preparing for a combat mission on 27 January, flying Jaguar XX962 'Fat Slags' in a four-ship with call sign Keeper 05. The target was a Silkworm site, which was obscured by weather and the alternate target, an ammunition and barracks site, was attacked instead. (*Courtesy A. Emtage*)

Alex continued about the performance of the aircraft:

> The laser on the aircraft, there were problems with the laser window. When we first started to go down the dive, we weren't getting a reliable ranging lock. It was an engineer, I think, who turned around and said, 'You have just spent the last two months flying around at 50ft and these lasers are getting sandblasted.'
>
> After the engineers worked their magic, we were then getting laser lock on at 25,000ft at a 40-degree dive. With a good ranging lock, stable conditions and a steady dive, weapon delivery could be remarkably accurate. One target was the elbow of a scrapyard that was being used as cover by the Iraqi forces, We put a CBU-87 in that from an 18,000ft drop. It became a more capable aeroplane as the war went on.
>
> Initially the CRV-7 weapon aiming was problematic. It would work on the range with Stevie T. and Frog working out the ballistics, but in a dynamic environment it was very hard to use. It was only when we got proper weapon aiming data utilising the laser that they could be reliably aimed.
>
> On one occasion I had to go to the spare jet. I started the engines and flipped the probe out for the engineers to inspect, the clips around it. The liney noticed a fault with the probe and said, 'You are not going.' I had to go for the spare; it must have been no more than ten minutes from check-in. I shut the engines down, put the pins in the seat and told the engineers, 'The rest of the aeroplane is yours.' We all had implicit trust in the guys that looked after the aircraft. At the spare I grabbed Alex Elliot who was seeing off the aircraft and said, 'I will do the weapons, the rest of the walk round is down to you.' I set the fusing to what I wanted, rushed into the cockpit, got everything set to go and he gave me the thumbs up. I made the check in because of him.
>
> There was a road that went across the runway at Muharraq. As soon as you crossed that road you would do a flares check and bounce them down the beach. At the time it seemed like a good idea; now that I think about it, maybe not!
>
> My father flew in the RAF for thirty-seven years and retired in 1990. He went on to be a technical author for BAE, working for Toby Craig's father. My father sent the baseball hat asking if I could have a photo taken with it and this was the result, only after I had demanded port and Stilton as a fee. My father sent me this parcel on 27 February, but it arrived in theatre after we had returned to the UK. The BFPO guys then sent it back, and it arrived on 41 [Squadron] late April. I remember a shout of, 'ET get down here and remove this parcel, it stinks.' They were right, it did! All that travelling had ripened it nicely. Port was good though.

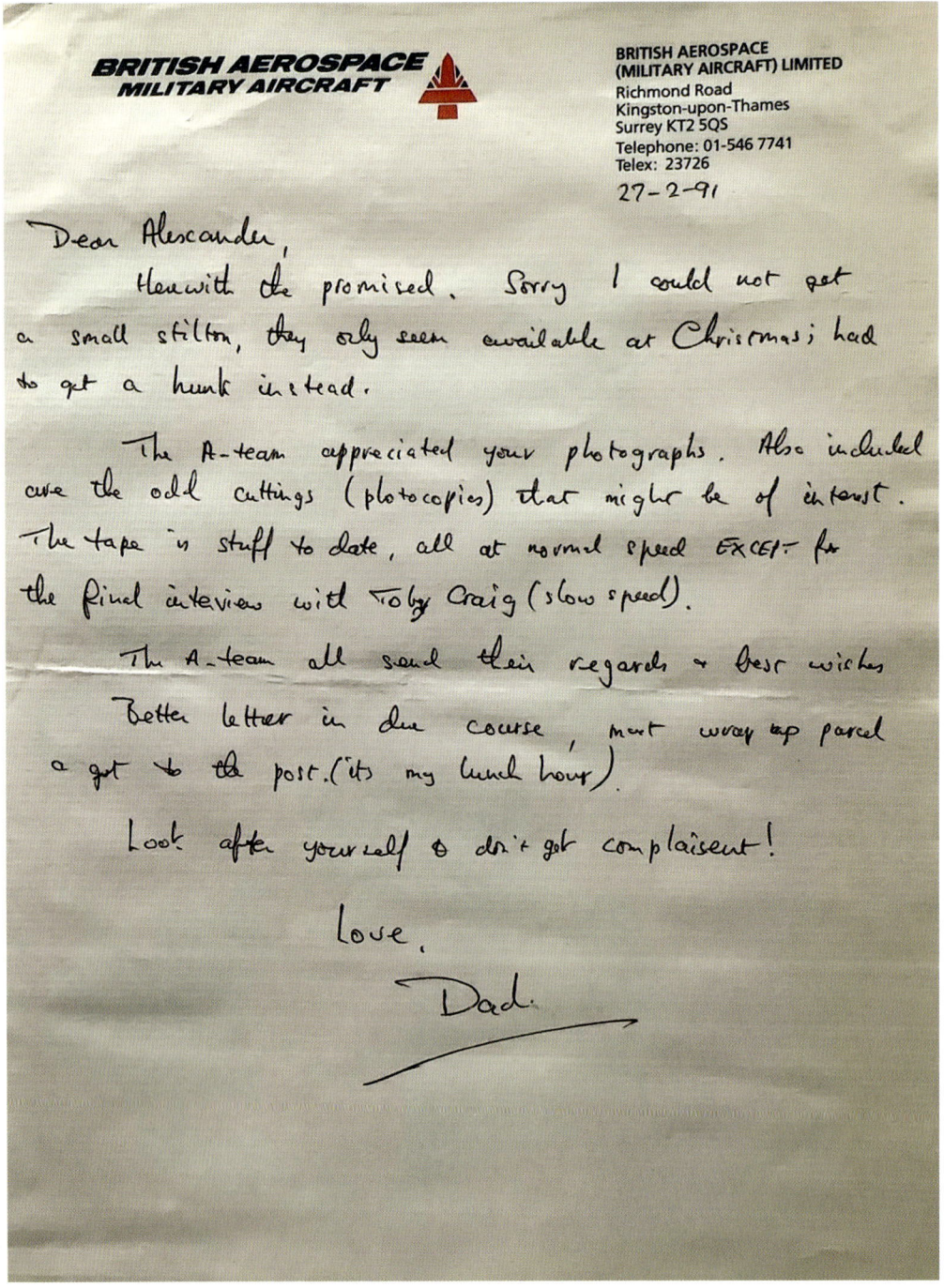

A letter from Flight Lieutenant Alex Emtage's father with reference to Stilton cheese. (*Courtesy A. Emtage*)

L–R: Flight Lieutenant Mark Hopkins, Squadron Leader Mike Rondot, Flight Lieutenants Mike Seares and Alex Emtage. (*Courtesy 41 Sqn ground crew*)

Flight Lieutenant Alex Emtage having just returned from a combat mission flying Jaguar XZ375, Guardian Reader. (*Courtsey of A. Emtage*)

Alex reflected on returning home and adjusting to the normality of routine life and having served on combat operations:

> Probably stranger for me was the transition to peace! Yes, we got pissed in Bahrain courtesy of GMTV etc, and there was military fanfare on our arrival home. It was more the expectation from me that other people's outlooks might have changed post-conflict … and obviously it had not, it was just a news article. Hit me hard once in a supermarket and took a long time to get used to.

## Squadron Leader Mike (Strike) Gordon

> You don't know what it is going to be like until you are doing it and you are learning all the time. No matter what people do to prepare you for it and not counting what you have done in training, nothing can compare.

Mike had the privilege to lead the first combat mission of the Jaguar force on 17 January, flying Jaguar XZ106 'Rule Britannia', call sign Bowler 51 flight, with his No 2 Flight Lieutenant Stevie Thomas, No 3 Flying Officer Mal Rainier and No 4 Flight Lieutenant Roger Crowder. The target was an Iraqi command post:

> In my four, I remember Steve and I took off together with me leading. When you get airborne you go into battle formation and Mal and Roger did the same. We were offset battle and that is so we could test the guns. I said, 'Let's test the guns.' I am sure I did it in a much higher, squeaky voice. The next thing I saw was a bloody missile flying past the cockpit and I heard Roger Crowder come up on the radio and say, 'Oops'. He had a switch pigs and selected missile instead of guns. The AIM-9 went soaring off into the middle distance. We had been airborne about a minute and we had nearly shot one of our own down! It's a mistake any one of us could have made and just shows the level of pressure we were all under.

Mike continued to describe the mission:

> There was what looked like a command post, which I attacked and then I saw some trucks. I had lost sight of Steve as the weather was not great and I selected the guns. It is amazing how quickly the guns empty when the adrenalin flows and I thought 'bugger this' and went around again. This time I fired an AIM-9 at them. My abiding memory of this was two things. The first was how stupid

it was: and the second, the missile just went soaring off and did not lock onto anything and went off into the desert. I did consider firing a second but thought I had wasted enough of the Queen's money at this point. That was a rule, never re-attack. It was an exciting first mission. I am not sure I hit anything; all I can say is the adrenalin was there.

Mike recalled the type of missions that would be flown and how personal perception changed about flying in combat:

We had different types of sorties where we would go to a dedicated kill zone, and anything that moved in that area you could attack. Then it was a combination of direct target attacks, which was CAP, going around with the tanker, round, and round in cycles, once we were up two and a half hours before we were called to a target.

There was one occasion when Stevie was leading one of the missions, his bombs didn't release; his recovery from the dive was much too shallow. The bombs had not released and I could see flak going off behind him. So, I flew back down, then chaffed and flared behind him and followed him back into the cloud. You don't think about anything apart from, it looks like he is in a bit of trouble. What do you do, look after yourself or your mate? He would have done exactly the same for me. Most people would have said it was stupid, even Steve would have, but it felt the right thing to do at the time. When I got back and thought, 'Would I have done things differently' and the answer would be yes, but at the time you do things to the best of your ability.

I felt a lot more vulnerable up high, and I was out of my comfort zone for a lot of the time. You don't know what kind of missiles the enemy has or what type of fighters they have, whether indeed they are going to employ them, so it's all of the unknown. At low level, in your comfort zone, you know what you can hit and what you can't. You know the rules about flying, you fly low enough to maintain a good lookout but you don't fly so low that you are next to your shadow. You look at the position of the sun for your ingress and your egress, you look at the terrain when you come into a target to get the best possible cover, right up to the point you need to pop to get your release height. When you are up at medium level you can see the target ten minutes away. The lookout is different when you are flying in a four-ship. At low level it tunnels a little because you are focusing on what is ahead of you. So, you are scanning much faster around, and you are reliant on the other guys. When you are high you have got another dimension because you are also looking down.

An over-wing AIM-9L in the foreground with Jaguar XX725 'Johnny Fartpants' at dispersal. This model of air-air missile is what was fired in error on the first Jaguar combat mission flown on 17 January. (*Source J. Lake*)

Squadron Leader Mike Gordon seated in the cockpit of Jaguar XZ106 'Rule Britannia' on 17 January. It is written in the squadron diary, 'The photograph was taken just prior to the mission, the expression on the pilots' faces speaks volumes.' (*Courtesy M. Gordon*)

On 1 February Mike was flying in Jaguar XX748, leading an eight-ship, callsign Keeper 01. This time flying at medium level helped him locate the target, al-Jaber airfield in Kuwait. He noticed how the smaller targets weren't always destroyed by heavy weapons:

> The easiest target was the airfield, you could see that miles away, the hardest was the Silkworm site on the coast but the boss said he had seen some pictures of it after the war and it was peppered with holes.

Mike was always impressed how the RAF tanker force supported the Jaguar fleet, remembering the excellent service they provided throughout the conflict:

> The tanker guys were absolutely amazing! Normal tanking is 25,000ft to 27,000ft. These guys would say, 'Where do you want the tow line?' I remember Baggers and Livo refuelling at 3,000ft in really bad weather over the desert. The tanker had come down to them. I also remember coming up to a tanker and getting overtaken by two US Navy aircraft saying they were desperate! They plugged into our tanker while we sat on the wing watching!!

Squadron Leader Mike Gordon and Flying Officer Mal Rainier conducting post-mission paperwork. (*Courtesy M. Rainier*)

A constant worry for pilots would be having to eject over a hostile combat zone, carrying only a pistol for personal protection:

> Mike Rondot did not like the PPK: it was a little pop gun that could not kill anyone, and he would not fly without a Browning, he said, if he was going to have a gun, he wanted one that could kill something. My feeling was that I could not hit a barn door at 10m with a Walter PPK so a Browning is not going to help. What good would it do anyway? Throw it at them!

Having leadership that was well respected by all pilots made the task of flying in combat much easier and Mike believes this was due to the boss, Wing Commander Bill Pixton:

> It was leadership on an exceptional level, Bill not only allowed me to lead the first mission but it was the level of responsibility he gave to everybody. He did not make any operational decisions without talking to someone. If it were something to do with weapons he would talk to the QWIs, if it were something around tactics he would also involve the squadron leaders. But still the weight of decision-making was on Bill's head.

The Gulf War was a stepping stone to how the UK military think today, how they employ their combat aircraft. But also, how legacy-type aircraft played an important role during this conflict, he recalls:

Squadron Leader Mike Gordon. (*Courtesy M. Gordon*)

The Gulf war changed completely the way we think, from the Cold War to modern warfare. I noticed it. Everything I had done in the UK and Germany was sort of wrong, this was a new way of thinking. Like the Tornado, went from JP233 straight and level over a runway getting the shit shot out of them, then to thinking we will lob bombs from a distance. Then to precision targeting from medium level with LGBs. On some missions, the Buccaneer had to spike for the Tornado and refuel the Tornado on the way back from the target, so here was the oldest aircraft in the fleet showing what the oldest aircraft can do!

Mike was awarded the DFC for his service during the Gulf war, gazetted on 29 June 1991.

## Flight Lieutenant Mark (Hoppy) Hopkins
Mark recalling his first combat mission in detail. On 19 January, he was flying Jaguar XX725 'Johnny Fartpants' as part of an eight-ship, call sign Keeper 01 flight.

The weather was poor, Stevie T was leading. As we got to the area crossing the border into Kuwait it was still poor, and I thought, are we going to go or turn back? At which stage Stevie put us in trail, and the other pair in TACAN trail and we went as pairs at 30 seconds in cloud. Stevie went down the dive first and came out of the cloud, and found what we were looking for, an SA-2 site. He was able to tell us there was sufficiently good weather so we pressed on. Alex and I both came out of cloud and ended up in trail and that was the last I saw of him. I got back to Bahrain on my own. Having dived on the SA-2 and released, as I turned back towards Saudi my RWR lit up like a Christmas tree! I quickly worked out what that was, which was all the coalition fighters locking me up to see if I was friend or foe. We were doing what we should never have done. We were silhouetted against an overcast, so they could visually see us from the ground, so it was time to get the hell out of there quickly before the anti-aircraft gunners got lucky. At this stage I ditched both tanks to give me better performance to get back into cloud.

Having landed safely back at al-Muharraq, Mark was met by members of the worldwide press, who were keen to talk to him about his first combat sortie:

I taxied in, spending a bit of the time getting my kit together, and when I came down the ladder, I got confronted by a TVAM Film Crew. The question was, 'What was it like to be back?' I thought, 'What a stupid question', and I forget exactly what I ended up saying. I said something like, 'Knowing that someone was shooting at you and trying to kill you is a pretty frightening experience.' The only bit that ended up on TV was, 'It was a pretty frightening experience.' I remember thinking at the time, 'You have misquoted what I said.' We all quickly turned around and said we are not going to allow the TV crews near until people have had time to get themselves mentally sorted.

By the time I had this conversation with the TV crew there was a centre-line fuel tank on the jet. I turned around and said to the ground crew, 'I thought I dropped that tank', and he said, 'We put a new one on, sir! Quick eh!'

It was not uncommon for the Jaguar to jettison its fuel tanks on combat sorties and he well remembers this procedure:

Bill said to us in a briefing at one stage, 'Remember they are called drop tanks for a reason! They are not keep tanks.' You normally needed to lift a spring-loaded cover to selectively jettison a store from a hardpoint, rather than clear the entire aircraft in an emergency. The springs were taken off so you could ditch them quickly. There were times when you needed better turn and climb performance to get away if the flak was heavy.

Mark described how he realised he had fired off an AIM-9L Sidewinder by mistake during this mission:

On the way back to base we would do buddy-buddy checks, which were battle damage checks. E.T. did the one on me and I then did one on him. I got the thumbs up and I asked if he noticed anything different? He replied 'no'. I said

L–R: Flying Officer Mal Rainier, Flight Lieutenants Roger Crowder, Stevie Thomas and Mark Hopkins. (*Courtesy M. Rainier*)

to look at the top of my right wing and all I got back from E.T. was 'bugger'. It was a very simple switch – in the centre was guns, right was right missile, left was left missile. In the heat of the moment, tipping in, I completely forgot I needed to move it as I was going to strafe some fast-moving patrol boats, having already fired on them with rockets. Later on, very kindly the ground crew presented me with an AIM-9 umbilical cord with 'Aden gun substitute' on a label attached to it.

On 24 February flying Jaguar XZ106 'Rule Britannia', call sign Keeper 01, he was leading an eight-ship (2 Planned 4 Ship missions on the same target) on a combat sortie. The target was a large SAM site, consisting of mixed SAM-2s, 6s and 8s, and other artillery targets located in southern Iraq, believed to be a Republican Guard position. He took off at 0845hrs and landed back at 1030hrs after a planned refuel from two Victor tankers.

> The weather was bad. I remember calling up the AWACs and getting on the tanker freq. We were eight aircraft planned against two Victor tankers. I asked where they were. He gave us a bearing and range from bullseye. I put it on my kneeboard, and he was nowhere near where he should be. Then I worked out his height was base minus. They were down at 2,000ft over the desert. This was the only clear airspace around, and they were nowhere near where they were meant to be, and at a height we were not used to. I put the eight-ship in two finger-four close formations in a minute trail on TACAN, which at that stage was 4 to 5 miles apart. Doing some mental gymnastics, I broke out of cloud at 3,000ft and over the desert south of the Iraqi border and thinking, 'Where are these guys!' With a speed and time calculation I thought he should be coming up on my right side, then almost on cue, two Victor tankers came right to left out of the murk. Luck or skill – I didn't mind, I'll take either. We slotted each four-ship in behind a tanker at 2,000ft. I was on the front tanker of course and Mike Rondot and I started to close on the basket. The fuel hoses were thrashing around a bit being at that low altitude, but we both made contact. However, the seal around the probe failed. I ended up with fuel from the tanker going down my right-hand engine because it was leaking out of the connection at this stage. The cockpit filled with an acrid sort of smoke, which was the fuel going down the engine and coming through the cockpit air conditioning feed. At this stage I disconnected in some speed and sitting there with eyes streaming just able to see the aircraft in front. I turned around to Mike and said the right-hand hose is trashed. We came home because we were out of time to get us to the target, I handed the lead to someone else and they pressed onto the target successfully.

Jaguar aircraft receiving fuel from a Victor tanker, an event similar to when the refuelling incident occurred on a combat mission on 24 February. (*Courtesy 41 Sqn, RAF*)

Flight Lieutenant Mark Hopkins taxiing back at RAF Coltishall in Jaguar XX748 after arriving from Bahrain on the completion of combat operations on 13 March 1991. The return journey, known as the 'leopard trail', took eight and a half hours with eleven air-to-air refuelling slots. (*Courtesy 41 Sqn, RAF*)

On returning to base Mark wrote in the remarks column of the authorisation sheets. '1 hose 1 victor + face full of AVTUR.'

Mark recalled with humour the day a senior RAF officer came to visit the squadron at al-Muharraq in the days just before the war started:

> We walked in for this speech meant to be a rousing moment for the troops. We are all in this coffee bar at al-Muharraq airbase. The room came to attention, but the first thing he was worried about was his hat and where he could put it. The next thing he says to Bill is, 'Are we secure in here?' No sir was the answer, so he starts to whisper! Now whispering he talks about how extremely exhilarating this experience will be for us and there was a wise crack from the back … exhilarating sir, you can have my maps! No sign of a rousing call to battle, which was a bit disappointing.

Flight Lieutenant Mark Hopkins.
(*Courtesy M. Hopkins*)

## Flight Lieutenant Peter (Livo) Livesey

Deploying on 1 January, Pete went out initially as the squadron's operations officer:

> I was on the OCU at the time, we weren't being used. It ended up with me and Bob Neilson as the two guys. Going down to Brize and a flight out to Riyadh and then jump in the back of an empty Herc and dropped off in Bahrain. There was me and this other lad who was going out to one of the Tornado squadrons and I remember walking off the back of this Herc, and nobody had told me a damn thing what was going on. I just wandered round and finally there was Chris Allam, walking towards me and he just looked at me and said, 'What are you doing here.' I turned around and said, 'Well I was rather hoping you were going to tell me actually!' They weren't expecting me. I don't think they knew who was coming out, was the impression I got. That was it and I started to do the ops job.

Pete remembers being sent out on combat operations to carry out a job that he had never trained to do:

> I sat in that briefing room; I had no idea what to do. Not a clue! We did the night shift, someone had to be there twenty-four hours a day. I was on duty the day the first Tornado went down; they had the same briefing facility as us. I remember when they all went over that first night and then when we realised it had all kicked off!

It was soon decided by Wing Commander Pixton that the Jaguar detachment needed dedicated reconnaissance pilots for specific recce missions:

> Billy P suggested to somebody up the chain, what about some recce assets. They said they didn't have any. Him turning around and saying, 'Well we have!' When the recce job came out they thought long and hard about it and it was decided Baggers would go. They needed someone to go with him, and I had already worked with the squadron, so they knew me, and I happened to be out there, so Bill asked me if I wanted to fly, and I said yes! Anything to get out of that ops room!

Not having much time to get accustomed to the missions and flying the jet in combat, he recalls one occasion with humour:

> Billy gave me a flight in a jet when I first got out there, we did a bit of OLF and HE strafe. There was a raft being towed by some naval boat. It was the funniest

thing I had seen in my life. Coming in at 100ft and starting a HE strafe. The only way you can stay on the target is pitch down. All hell is breaking loose in front of you, and all you are doing is pitching into the water. At 100ft it is getting a little bit tense and I thought to myself, 'You better stop now.' You are having that much fun! The thing about the Aden cannon was it was the most ridiculous aircraft to have to have a bloody gun in it. If you fired one of them it was alright, you fired two you couldn't see anything, you had blurred vision because the whole cockpit was vibrating.

Pete's first combat mission was on 11 February flying Jaguar XZ356, 'Mary Rose'. He was carrying a F126 LOROP pod and his lead was Squadron Leader Dave Bagshaw, their call sign Longstop 11. Their mission was to take photos of an Iraqi artillery position.

The recce side of things was fine, going in medium level, nothing below 15,000ft, even with the centre-line recce pod on at that altitude it took better pictures. It was a very narrow field of view. You could not just randomly take pictures of things, you had to line it up. I always had a specific target. Initially you set off just looking for AAA, they put the guns in trenches, that's where you found that sort of stuff. There was a little bit of AAA but not that much. I remember flying back, north of the city, and I was just looking at the ground, and in a big lazy turn going out to sea. I just saw this flash down on the ground. I thought to myself, 'I wonder what that is?' There was these bursts of smoke a couple 1,000ft below me and it was AAA. It looked just like fireworks going off.

I always said, 'Me and Baggers went to war thirteen times together, and never came back together!' I was on the LOROP camera, which was massive! Baggers would be seeing things, over here, over there. Eventually, Baggers where are you? Not having radar, so once we lost visual of each other we were two singletons. I would come up and say, 'I am off home.'

The LOROP camera, Baggers had that one this day. It's not weighty, it's just real draggy. Baggers did not like going high on take-off. We took off one day and I was looking down at him. We both rotated, we put the gear up, and he ran one of the tires down the runway with it halfway up. How it did not knacker the back of the pod going down the runway God knows!

Pete commented on the performance of the Jaguar:

I don't think it is an unfair to statement to say, but the Jaguar is a most maligned aeroplane. Good old Brits, let's take that heap of French rubbish and we will do something with it. They actually turned it into something and gave it a role, and

Flight Lieutenant Pete Livesey preparing for a mission piloting Jaguar XZ358 'Diplomatic Service'. This aircraft regularly carried the F126 recce pod fit. (*Courtesy P. Tholen*)

it actually became very good at what it did. Nobody likes to admit that. It went from A to B low level; it dropped bombs and came back. It was only when you started adding things onto it. For example, we were overhead a SAM-9 happily, at 450 knots, low level. It was the smallest aircraft you had ever seen. Even when you were doing 2,000yd, line abreast, half the time you could not see the guy next to you. It's not your eyesight, it is just this thing is so damn small!

Pete was based at Muharraq, with the airfield protected by the RAF Regiment with the Rapier missile system. However, it seemed they were more of a deterrent than an active threat on a few occasions, as he recalls.

At the end of the runway they had these Rapiers, because of the elevation of the missile, and having never been used, when they left them there, whatever held the missile on, it stopped, and these missiles were just sliding off the back. So, they ended up, they were actually tied on with string. How true this was I don't know but this was the story that went around. Another time, there had been a couple of practice air raids, and this Regiment officer decided our reaction was not good enough. So, he decided to start throwing thunder flashes around. I am not sure he was there at the end of that day.

## Squadron Leader Richard (Dick) Midwinter

At the end of November 1990, Dick arrived in Bahrain via RAF Akrotiri on a C-130. He started training for low-level tactics up to his departure: 'Right up to three days before we went to war we were training low level.'

Dick's first mission was on 19 January, flying Jaguar XZ364 'Saddam' as part of an eight-ship formation with call sign Keeper 01:

It was an SA-2 site; they had got the bigger range in those days. Most of it was in cloud in close formation going into a war zone, you see all this lightning. Oh, come on, wake up, it's not lightning. Then you dive out of the cloud onto the target and back into cloud when you come off.

I remember the day the cloud all cleared up; you could see all these aircraft heading the same way as you. We were meant to climb out of Bahrain and climb to height, staying in our corridor. We made the border at the height we were meant to be in the corridor, and it wasn't until you saw everyone else and wondered if you had gone through their corridor on the way.

Remembering the Jaguar and its combat performance, he said:

We removed the guards of the selective jettison buttons after I got a hang up, three 1,000lb bombs went, but one stayed on and immediately you begin to roll.

I did not want to get rid of everything at this stage, at 20,000ft. There were spring catches. You are flying with your right hand, but the selectors are on the right-hand side of the cockpit. You swap hands, try and try and get the flap up to press the button underneath it. Meantime, I am still rolling. I did jettison the bomb. Otherwise it would have meant getting rid of everything. Simon had a missile fired at him and he jettisoned everything. It was a good aim; I am sure he saw it. I shouted at him. He came back with wires hanging out of his pylons. The RWR pod and chaff dispenser, you could not jettison these. In wartime stick some armed carts in there and you can get rid of the lot! We were flying straight forward dumb 1,000-pounders to start with, then when the Tornados started taking the hits using low-level tactics they took all of our 1,000-pounders. We presumed the enemy were visually aiming at us. The Jaguar is quite small. We were sure they were visual aiming SAMs at us. Anyone looking up at you would not see you; if you use flares on the attack they could go, 'Oh, there is an aircraft.' We used a lot of flares when we got out of Bahrain to test the system. The SA-7 you could not do anything about until someone fired it at you.

On 31 January Dick was flying Jaguar XX748 in a two-ship formation as call sign Batsman 02, with Flight Lieutenant Simon Young as lead. Taking off to conduct SUCAP, they took position over predesignated airspace and waited for orders:

Squadron Leader Dick Midwinter and Flight Lieutenant Dick MacCormac walking to their aircraft preparing for a combat sortie. (*Courtesy S. Young*)

> The two of us took BL755s on a mission, which we ended up using. I told Bill before we went it was a bad idea and when I got back I am not doing that again. If we are going to go in the same way we would do normally then plan it, drop it fine. Doing it from a medium-level CAP is pointless unless you are going to drop into low level properly instead of, 'Here is the target and go and hit it.' We were using them on SUCAP. Sat up getting fuel from a tanker and if they wanted us to go in and have a go at something we would. It was that day they thought the Iraqis were advancing along a road. Simon and I were on CAP and there was a classic switch pigs. I was on a different radio frequency at some stage to Simon so when he was getting briefed on what they wanted us to do it was late on that I picked up what it was that we actually needed to do. It was going down to hit a ZSU-234. Get in over the sea low level before you go into the war zone and hit the ZSU-234. Not only that, we went in separate, one keeping top cover when the other guy went in to hit the target. To go from medium level to low level and get it all right and not practising, it was just a disaster waiting to happen! Simon managed to hit a ZSU-234, mine went way short to where it was meant to go. It was one of those classic things you read about in all previous wars, why did we change this mid-war? CRV-7 was the way to go, if we had these then we would have had a look at the road and picked our targets.

Reflecting on the use of this method and type of attack, Dick believed it was ordered from higher command to utilise this type of weapon system:

> 'Go and use them', that was the reason. You have been trained to use it! Hang on we have been flying at medium level for weeks and now you want us to go back in with no practice at low level and use these.

One night in the Diplomat while in bed:

> The first air raid siren that went off in the hotel, we all went down to the basement, nothing happened. We all thought, 'Hang on a minute we are all knackered, got up, gone down to the basement, sat there with gas masks, and done nothing. Actually, next time I am going to stay in bed!'

Dick said about the Jaguar force routine during the Gulf War:

> We got it set up really well and, hats off to Bill, we did four days and had a day off. We flew once in a day and we could have kept going. Certainly, at some stage they said when the next roulement would be. We said, 'We are here and will finish the job.' You could see by that stage it would be fairly short.

Squadron Leader Dick Midwinter and Flight Lieutenant Simon Young relaxing completing post-mission paperwork at dispersal. (*Courtesy S. Young*)

## Wing Commander William (Bill) Pixton, AFC

When orders were issued that the UK would deploy air forces in support of likely operations in Iraq, Wing Commander Pixton was deployed on the Reconnaissance Air Meet (RAM) 90, a competition in Texas:

> I wasn't on the RAM 90 team per se; I simply went along as the Sqn Boss and to socialise. After a week or so, once that novelty had worn off, I bade my farewells and hitched a ride on a VC10 back to the UK. Shortly after arriving home I was watching the six o'clock news and across the television screen taxied a 41 Squadron Jaguar. The reporter said it was going to deploy to Oman in the next few days. This clearly got my attention! Instead of taking a week off as I had planned, I put on my flying suit and drove into work at RAF Coltishall. Wing Commander Jerry Connolly, OC 6 Squadron, had already identified twelve aircraft and the appropriate number of pilots for the deployment, including a reconnaissance element from 41 Squadron. The Station Commander was on leave at the time, so Jerry was not only the leader of the deployment, he was also the acting Station Commander. He was surprised to see me as he thought I was still in the States. I asked if there was anything I could do. 'Nope', was the reply and 'you can wave us goodbye!' A few days later, twelve pink jets took off, did a fly-by, and went off to Oman.

To start with, there was no talk of follow-on support or of a roulement. It was assessed that operations would commence fairly soon and the deployed Jaguar aircraft would do their bit and return home once hostilities ended. However, it soon became apparent that this was not going to be the case and there was now a need to establish a second effective fighting unit drawn from the Jaguar Force as a whole. Wing Commander Pixton needed similar numbers of pilots and aircraft to those that had deployed on the first wave. However, there were issues from the start. The first deployment had taken the majority of the Coltishall Squadron's Qualified Weapons Instructors (QWIs). Understandably, the first wave had also taken the lion's share of the more experienced pilots on the Wing.

> I was left with a number of two-ship leaders, not many four-ship leaders, and certainly no eight-ship leaders, apart from myself. I also had to find two QWIs. I was a QWI, as was one of my remaining flight commanders, Chris Allam, but we were rather busy being the boss and flight commander respectively. I put out a plea across the Jaguar Force and Pete Tholen, who was just about to leave the Air Force, and Stevie Thomas, a QWI on the OCU, answered the call. Both were put on the list straight away. I had also lost my executive officer to the first go, leaving me just two flight commanders and I needed a third. This slot was filled by Squadron Leader Mike Rondot from 6 Squadron.

Wing Commander Pixton arrived in Bahrain on 3 December 1990 and was the last pilot of the Jaguar Roulemont to arrive in theatre. 'I flew in with 41 Squadron's troops in a C-130, we got out and 6 Squadron got in and flew off. That said, I did get a one-night handover with Jerry.' Squadron Leader Mike Gordon was instrumental in drafting the daily flying programme, and it soon became obvious that two waves a day would be optimal and sustainable with twenty-two operational pilots. This would enable us to programme two pilots as a recce pair, sixteen pilots to fly four x four ship attack sorties and four pilots on stand-down daily.

> To achieve this flying programme I needed another seven pilots on top of those that arrived in the roulement. There were two pilots who had deployed with Jerry; Mal Rainier and Nick Collins. They had already done their three months stint in the desert but they were young flying officers and single, so I asked them if they would like to stay on! One of the guys said yes straight away, and the other said yes, having slept on it. I also had two ops officers who were Jaguar pilots; one was Pete Livesey, an ex No2 (AC) Sqn Jaguar recce pilot. It just so happened that I needed a wingey with recce experience for Baggers, who I decided was going to lead the recce pair. I asked Livo, 'do you fancy flying?' He replied 'absolutely'.

A minor issue was that Livo hadn't refuelled air-to-air in his life, so Baggers taught him how to air-to-air refuel on combat missions. This still left me four short so I contacted Coltishall and asked for reinforcements. I was sent a flight commander, Dick Midwinter, which was handy, Toby Craig, Simon Young and Dick MacCormac.

Headquarters in Riyadh tasked four-ships and sometimes eight-ships to begin with. However, we soon realised that only the first two aircraft in these formations benefited from the element of surprise during the attack while the rest of the formation tended to attract most of the flak. To fix this we reduced the formation size to two-ship only. The tasking became one recce pair and eight attack pairs for the rest of the campaign.

On 17 January, the first official day of the conflict, Wing Commander Pixton recalled in his diary:

> War has broken out. I can't believe it! It's 04.00 hrs local and the Kuwaitis are in the foyer of the hotel watching CNN like an insomniac football crowd.
>
> Jaguar pilots quite excited at the prospect and we wait our turn keenly, some more than others. 3rd Tornado wave gets airborne, still no Jaguar tasking. I am holding four Jaguars on 30 minutes readiness for CSAR. Four on 30 minutes Ground alert, Close Air Support and four on 60 minutes GCAS. CNN in the briefing room is like the Ben Hur epic.
>
> 1st Tornado lost. It looks like they got out but the mood in the squadron has changed, much more subdued. I am offered the first Jaguar tasking by Riyadh and told I have a choice whether to accept or not! This is unbelievable and an unexpected responsibility. It dawns on me that the fate of the Jaguar pilots rests largely on my shoulders, wibble. With some trepidation, I accept the CAS tasking. Give it to Mike Gordon's four ship flying as call sign Bowler 51 flight, consisting of Flight Lieutenants Steve Thomas, and Roger Crowder, and Flying Officer Mal Rainier, they are the ones holding the 30-minute GCAS slot, and I go off to worry.

Wing Commander Pixton's first combat mission was on 18 January 1991, flying as four-ship lead with call sign Bowler 51 and piloting XX725 'Johnny Fartpants'. Within the formation were Flight Lieutenants Pete Tholen and Ted Stringer and Flying Officer Nick Collins.

> I was leading a four-ship CAS/AI mission and our tasked target was in Kuwait but when we reached the tasked target area the weather was so socked in we couldn't see the ground. So, instead of turning for home, stupidly, I called up the

AWACs and said, 'Here we are, I have four jets with bombs but no target because ours is weathered out.' The AWACS replied, 'Oh great, I got an A-10 in Iraq who has found a Republican Guard outfit and he needs some guys with MK 82s.'

I replied, 'I've not got MK 82s but pretty close, Brit 1,000-pounders, equivalent to a US Mk83' and 'Fine, we are up for that.'

There were only three rules I gave to the pilots: we would not fly below 15,000ft, we would not re-attack and we would not fool (spoon) around in enemy territory. To see the ground on this occasion, we would likely have to descend well below 15,000ft, and it would be spooning around in enemy territory because we didn't know precisely what we were looking for! And we probably would have to fly a few re-attacks because we would likely be unable to find whatever it was. BUT, being the first trip of a real war, it's kind of tough to just go home fully bombed up! The AWACs gave us the lat and long of the estimated target location and told us that the A-10 needs our HELP, which is a very emotive word really. This bloke was obviously a fast FAC and on his own in enemy territory. Off we went to help. It turned out that the cloud base in Iraq was down at about 10,000ft, which was 5,000ft lower than I wanted to go. We were now in pairs trail in cloud, with Ted Stringer and Nick Collins behind and Pete Tholen on my wing. I made contact with the A-10 and he described that he had popped out of cloud at 11,000ft or so, found some 'Republican Guard' units which he had marked with his 'Willie Pete' smoke rockets. However, as soon as he came out of cloud, 'everyone' started shooting at him, so he turned away and went back into cloud, which I thought was pretty reasonable. We decided that he would come in from the west and after breaking cloud he would again mark the targets with smoke rockets and turn away back to west. We would approach from the south, pop out of cloud at about 10,000ft see the smoke on the targets and drop our bombs on them and turn away back to the south. Thinking about it afterwards, the chances of this plan happening were pretty small to zero. His A-10 wasn't equipped with a laser marker so we were relying on smoke rockets only. We were planning to pop out of the cloud doing 450kts, heading north while he's doing 300kts heading east all heading for the same spot. The biggest chance is that there's going to be a big clang as we hit each other. The adrenalin was up and I didn't want to go home with four full aircraft. Now getting to the vinegar stroke, we had the lat and long of the target in the nav kit, the timing circle in the HUD was running down, with a minute left to go, all the weapon switches to green and ready to pickle the bombs. I'm going to select CCIP once we break cloud. Descending through 11,000ft, the A-10 pops out of cloud at the correct time. Then the radio goes bananas, 'Shit I'm taking fire, swearing and blinding, knock it off, knock it off!' My adrenalin went up a level! I now have fifteen seconds to run to target, I can see the cloud breaking, now at 10,000ft. My wingy, Pete, in close formation, shouts, 'Boss, AAA'. This yellow flash comes between us, I saw it pop just above the fin of his aeroplane. Shit, I thought (right, pickle everything, NOW), we jettisoned everything we had live. Ten seconds to run to the inertial point, not seen the ground, didn't see his smoke rockets, everything fell off, I broke really hard right, 'poor old Pete, no way is he going to stay with me'. I was concerned they would have IR SAMs; I did not want to put the burners in, I figured that would give them a really good growl. I couldn't stop pulling, it was quite strange. We have a stall warner/alpha warner and a RWR audio warning, and they are quite similar. Both were blaring in my ears, there was something on the RWR, but I was not in a fit state to diagnose what it was. I realised I was about to lose control of the aeroplane. Pete, I've lost him in cloud, turning 90 degrees, going up 3,000 to 4,000ft, back in cloud, doing 180 knots, at 12 to 14 alpha, going nowhere. Pulling a bit more, finally managed to educate my right arm to let off a bit, jettisoned the tanks, I don't need two empty tanks. Bombs had gone, put the burners in. I staggered around 180 degrees to where I had come in from, climbed up to 15,000ft. By this time, I heard Ted and Nick saying on the radio, 'crossing the border', confirming they were out the country and back into Saudi. I still had 25 miles left to go. Pete was also across the border, 10 miles ahead of me, having flown his aircraft correctly.

All the flight managed to get back safely to al-Muharraq. On landing I checked the aircraft for damage. 'No damage at all, no marks or holes. The tracer must have popped far enough away.' In the debrief, I said to Pete, 'How do you know what AAA looks like? Because I don't? I sure do now! Guessing it was tracer from a weapon similar to the calibre as the Jaguar Aden cannon.'

An A-10C Thunderbolt, nicknamed the Warthog. This is the same type of aircraft that provided FAC(A) support to Bowler 51 flight on 18 January. (*Author's Collection*)

A keen smoker, Wing Commander Pixton devised a way to have a crafty cigarette in the cockpit while flying on long missions.

> When I was in the States flying A-10s on exchange, I noticed on one occasion that there was smoke in my leader's cockpit while we were in the arming bay. I called him on the radio and told him, 'It looks like you are on fire.' He replied, 'Shut up!' It transpired during the sortie debrief that he was a Vietnam veteran and on 'long trips' he really needed a drag. He explained that you must turn the oxygen off and an ash tray was essential. The gunsight camera film tins made good ash trays and the bungee cord over the coaming of the A-10 held it secure; the air conditioning is pretty calm up there too.
>
> Once, when we were coming back from a rather strenuous mission up north, I asked Pete, who was leading, if we could fly a bit lower.
>
> 'Why?', he replied
>
> 'I can't get a light.'

On landing, the engineers would often comment; 'Looks like we need to hoover this one out, there's ash all over the floor.'

Bill remembers preparing for a combat mission:

> Your first thought on waking up is to hope it's a clear blue day and then it is straight to work. Things begin to get a bit tense during briefing but it's not until you have your flying suit and lifejacket on and the maps under your arm and the instruction is given that you are to fly, that you really feel the tension. Then it is out to the plane, and lots of people wish you luck, and 'see you soon', and they get that look in their eye, which means they 'hope' they will see you soon, but you just laugh it off. You remain cool as you settle into the aircraft and concentrate on the job in hand. Once the engine starts it gets a bit sweaty, and you form a plan in your own mind of what you are going to do and in the back of your mind check what you do if you get hit.
>
> The rest is routine. Take-off, radio silence, flying over the sea and waiting to see the border of Kuwait distinctive in the desert sand, now you are on your own. Over the target, if you miss there is no point in going; that is the bottom line. Once you get to the border, which you can see as a line in the desert, you are looking out the window to see if there is anything coming up at you. You just see desert and a lot of smoke because it is burning quite well out there.
>
> By then you are at the stage where all concentration is on hitting the target. The main worry is that when you come to release the weapons the damn things don't go because you've made a mistake (switch pigs).

*Above and below*: Evidence of smoking in the cockpit while on long combat missions. It is written in the operational diary in relation to the last photo of Bill flying Jaguar XZ367 'White Rose': 'The boss caught having a crafty tab on the way home.'

Flight Lieutenant Edward Stringer recalls; 'Leading one mission back, it was coming towards the end and talking to the US Navy, trying to get back as fast and high as you could, and Bill asked if we could go lower, then even lower. I said, "Yes OK," and cleared it thorough Red Crown, the control agency. We dropped down to 10,000ft. I came up to the boss on the back radio and asked why down here and not at 32,000ft? He came alongside with his oxygen mask hanging off and said, 'Couldn't get a light up there!' (*Courtesy 41 Sqn, RAF*)

During the attack, you don't see the flak coming up at you, you get told by your wingman that you are being fired at. You log it and get to it when it is next in the queue because you still have five seconds to go. Actually, that is twenty-twenty hindsight. At the time you think: 'Oh shit, but come on its nearly time for bombs to go.' Time seems to stretch and the three seconds or so you have to aim the weapon and let it go seems an age.

It's a lifetime. It is amazing what you can do out there within a heartbeat, things that could never have been done in training. You look over your shoulder and see the weapons going off. Then it is 'get my little pink body home'. I've been told I am being shot at, so I sort that out, turning my chaff and electronic countermeasures on, and turn around and head for the border as high and as fast as I can.

Jaguar XZ356 'Mary Rose' at dispersal. (*Courtesy 41 Sqn, RAF*)

On 3 February, during one of these journeys back to base and just off the coast of Kuwait, I happened to fly high level over the battleship USS *Missouri* just as it fired a full broadside, four turrets, three barrels per turret. I believe the projectiles were the size of a car. You could see the ship move with the recoil. It was quite amazing to see!

On 30 January, flying XZ364 'Saddam' as call sign Longstop 01, with support from his No. 2, Flight Lieutenant Pete Tholen, Wing Commander Pixton successfully assisted in the destruction of a Polish-designed Polnocny C-class landing ship that was transiting near the mouth of the Shatt al-Arab waterway. It was assessed to have a maximum crew of forty-seven personnel, and rocket launchers on board. It had already been engaged by US Navy A-6 Intruders and the vessel was attempting to flee into Iranian territory waters. Bill wrote in his logbook 'life rafts in area'.

Wing Commander Bill Pixton flying Jaguar XZ119 'Katrina Jane' OLF over the water. Taken by Flight Lieutenant Pete 'Frog' Tholen. (*Courtesy P. Tholen*)

Three or four coalition AAR tankers were usually positioned over the Gulf in a racetrack pattern at various assigned altitudes. Our Victor was in this stack and on that day we had refuelled from him once already. Back on CAP, 'Red Crown' vectored us to a Polnocny-class LSL that was making a run across the gulf towards Iran. It had already been damaged by coalition air by the time we arrived. We proceeded to fly two rocket passes each and three or four guns passes each before heading back to the tanker. Five or six circuits/attacks of the target used much more fuel than the more usual single-pass attack, so we were a little short! Certainly not enough fuel to make it back to Bahrain. Fortunately, the tanker stack was on our way home. Once at the tanker racetrack we struggled to find the Victor due to the broken cloud at his level. The Victor crew had a wonderful time firing off Very flares from the pistol fitted to the cabin roof in a bid to catch our attention – the only opportunity they had to fire something in anger and filling the cockpit with cordite fumes to boot! By the time we finally spotted them we were a little short of fuel. As I approached the basket, the Victor coincidentally reached the end of his racetrack and called 'Turning left!' Clearly, plugging in in the turn is a little more difficult than straight and level, and 'difficult' was the last thing I needed at the time, so I replied, jokingly, 'If you turn I will shoot you!' The tanker captain immediately got the message and pressed straight on regardless of his designated tanker track. We both plugged in first time and the pressure dissipated.

A Polnocny C-class landing ship similar to the one engaged on 30 January. (*Courtesy Royal Navy archives*)

Wing Commander Bill Pixton preparing for a mission, in the first photo climbing into Jaguar XX725 'Johnny Fartpants', and in the second seated in the same aircraft. (*Courtesy W. Pixton and A. Emtage*)

At the end of each sortie, pilots would conduct a thorough debrief of the mission they had just carried flown:

> We would take some time debriefing the gunsight videos of the attack we had just flown to make sure our claims were accurate and that our tactics were effective.
> All the Jaguar pilots deployed to Bahrain were combat ready but with different lead status. I offered one or two pilots the opportunity to upgrade during the campaign from pairs leader to four-ship lead but interestingly they all declined.

Reflecting on command and how experience and training helped preparations for war, Wing Commander Pixton understood his pilots well:

> Nobody was going to kill themselves on purpose. We are in a combat environment now, you don't have to tell people to be careful. They are going to be. Flying is dangerous enough as it is but in combat operations it's clearly more so. However, it was noticeable that with no interference from me, everyone did their job well.

Wing Commander G.W. Pixton was awarded the DFC for his command and service during Gulf War 1, announced in *The London Gazette* on 29 June 1991.

Pilots' Personal Extracts 101

Bill seated in an unknown Jaguar, possibly XZ106 'Rule Britannia'. Note the AIM-9L Sidewinder on the bomb tally artwork. (*Courtesy W. Pixton*)

*Above*: Landing back at RAF Coltishall from combat operations on 13 March 1991. (*Courtesy 41 Sqn, RAF*)

*Right*: Wing Commander Bill Pixton standing next to his aircraft, Jaguar XZ356 'Mary Rose'. (*Courtesy W. Pixton*)

## Flying Officer Malcolm (Mal) Rainier

Mal and Flying Officer Nick Collins arrived into theatre early October 1990 as part of the initial Jaguar deployment, commanded by Wing Commander Jerry Connolly, OC 6 Squadron. His first memory was of the two pilots that were being replaced:

> We were replacing Flight Lieutenants Nick Connor and Rob Last. As we stumbled down the steps of the police post, I have never seen smiles broader. They were smiling like smiley things.

On settling into his new environment, intense training began with low-level sorties. It was soon understood that to conduct a standard interdiction mission to Kuwait and back would be in excess of five hours. To add, AAR assets were in short supply so the Jaguar force had moved earlier to Muharraq, Bahrain.

> The French Armée de l'Air arrived in October with their Jaguars at Al-Ahsa. This was somewhat closer than we were from the action, so we made a note to pop in should the need arise. As it happens it did, when one of our number left the 'partial throttle reheat' engaged, which rapidly left him short of fuel. Instead of Al Ahsa, he found an airstrip closer by to land on and seek fuel.

To add to the overall plan, it was soon realised that with a directive imposed of a ninety-day detachment limit, all the training that had been conducted up to this stage was in vain. Over the Christmas period replacement pilots from 41 Squadron were in place and Mal remained with them on request from Wing Commander Bill Pixton. This was due to extra pilots being required and also to ensure some continuity with the handover.

> We had a secret Santa, Baggers got a pair of binoculars, so he could spot the tanker, blind as a bat! We also had a moustache-growing competition. Mine was pretty poor, Shutty had one instantly, not me. Bum fluff. Footy was too cool to ever have a moustache.

The GR1A Jaguar was modified to deploy to Iraq with external and internal fittings. This enhanced its capability but added extra switches into the cockpit:

> Stuff had basically been glued on. There was a switch on the coaming that selected the function of the trigger. If you had the switch in the wrong position then the wrong munition would be fired when you pressed said trigger. For a guns attack, you could call up the gunsight in the HUD, turn the guns on, make the late-arm switch and pull the trigger. There was no indication that you'd made a mistake until the guns didn't fire but a £100k missile did. It was bad ergonomics and simple human frailty. This happened on a number of occasions and was so embarrasing.

*Above*: Flying low level over the desert, taken from the cockpit rear-view mirror. Note the AIM-9L Sidewinder on the over-wing rail. (*Courtesy M. Rainier*)

*Right*: Flying Officer Mal Rainier displaying his moustache-growing skills. (*Courtesy M. Rainier*)

Christmas 1990 at Muharraq, Bahrain. (*Courtesy M. Rainier*)

This came to fruition during the first Jaguar combat mission of the Iraqi conflict, of which Mal was a part, flying Jaguar XX725 'Johnny Fartpants' on 17 January as part of call sign Bowler 51 flight.

> The pre-match briefing on the evening of 16 January was a sobering affair. The Tornado boys were to penetrate at low level, at night, all the way to Saddam's strategic assets. The Jags were to be tasked in daylight over the most heavily defended part of the Kuwait Theatre of Operations, without dedicated SEAD. I remember murmuring to one of my mates on 15 Squadron, who were co-located at Muharraq, that I was, 'Glad I'm not a Tornado-mate.' He looked at me seriously and said, 'Glad I'm not a Jag-mate.'
>
> We were all champing at the bit on the first night, but it was clear that the 'night' raids were going to last until after dawn. As we strapped in, there was a good deal of tension because nobody knew what was coming. Unusually, Mr Cartwright climbed the steps of the jet that I was preparing to fly ostensibly to wish me luck, but as he left he said, 'Oh and it's a silent launch.' One bit of essential information that should perhaps have formed part of the briefing. I assumed that the formation would switch from ground to tower as we approached the runway, tower to approach after take-off and check in on the squadron chat frequency after take-off. He reassured me that I'd guessed correctly. There were plenty more surprises to come on that trip.
>
> Strike, Stevie T as No. 1 and 2, and myself and Roger Crowder as No. 3 and 4. We got airborne all with two-centre-line MF/BF fused bombs with Mk960 fuses and the Aden cannon loaded with belts of 120 rounds of four HE and four AP bullets. Our target was a police post on the border of Kuwait. We ingressed at around 16,000ft and egressed at around 18,000ft. Strike had read and understood the Air Tasking Order and we were (correctly as it turns out) at least as scared of our own side as the enemy. He thought we'd 'go with the flow', rather than leopard crawl all the way to and from the target. We all returned unharmed and with bags of fuel, however, various things happened. Roger manages to loosen off a missile by accident and nobody sees it apart from the tanker in the distance. We all think, the Iraqis are pretty close! I did not see it go off, but we did a battle damage check afterwards and he was missing a 'Winder!

There was a further incident that occurred on this combat sortie:

> My bombs had dropped off the aeroplane. As soon as one bomb-fuse armed, it went bang! I only found out chatting to Roger, my wingman, years after the event. He said that he'd seen a massive explosion behind my aircraft. He had thought it was AAA but actually it was one of the two bombs that I had dropped. The bomb has a selectable

Flying Officer Mal Rainier in the cockpit of a Jaguar. (*Courtesy M. Rainier*)

post-release arming time. We chose 4-5 seconds for the fuse to 'wake up' to give us time to pull clear as the old Mk947 and Mk952 fuses had a measurable risk of going off at arming (this was the fruit of years of in-service experience). The MFBF, which we used on the first raid, had been sold to us with a risk of fusing at arming of zero.

There was always the concern about having to bail out when flying over a hostile area in the Gulf War, and Mal remembers in detail.

> The whole E & E [escape and evasion] thing, it was going to be a long walk. There were bugger all features out there, and you had to head east to the sea. You might get lucky and meet a local that might not slot you.

Mal made the national newspapers for a remark that was caught in an interview on returning from a combat sortie. With a shy grin, he said, 'I didn't stay around too long, I was more concerned about running away bravely.'

Having time to relax was important and being accommodated at the Diplomat Hotel meant this was possible. Being the youngest Jaguar pilot, Mal was often tasked to organise entertainment evenings and inviting the fellow RAF squadrons.

> We had the Tornado guys down the road in another hotel. We had joint parties, we would arrange once or twice on the top floor of the Diplomat a few drinks and some food, Tornado and Jag. Then all your peers that you went through training with would turn up. When we started to lose people early on in the conflict it was all the tougher because we had just been socialising with them.

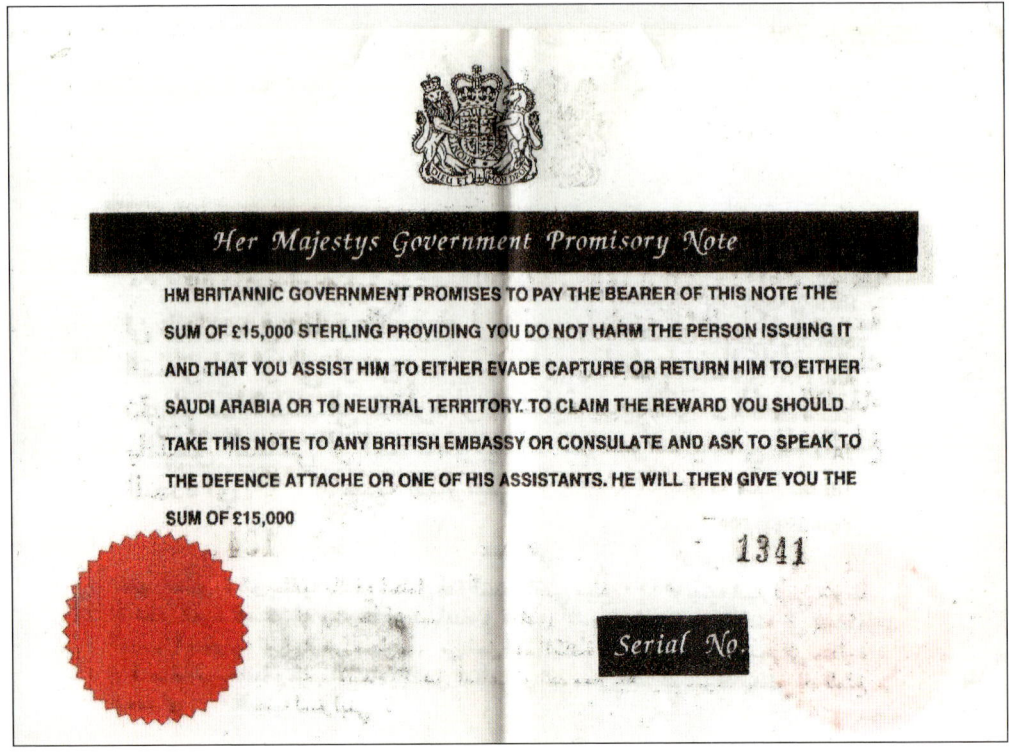

A goolie chit carried by Flying Officer Mal Rainier. If an airman had to bail out in hostile territory this chit could be shown to a local civilian to ask for assistance and, if needed, medical aid. A financial reward would be given when the downed pilot reached friendly lines. Arabic was written on the reverse. (*Courtesy M. Rainier*)

Flying Officer Mal Rainier and Flight Lieutenant Roger Crowder. (*Courtesy M. Rainier*)

Mal in XX725 'Johnny Fartpants' on 17 January preparing to deploy on the Jaguar's first Gulf War combat mission. (*Courtesy M. Rainer*)

On one occasion an air-to-air engagement nearly occurred with Iraq fighters:

> Every fourth trip, we were tasked to provide support CAP, which involved going to a tow line out just off the coast and awaiting tasking, dipping into the AAR towline assets when required. These missions could last up to four hours and tasks included attacking the Iraqi feint towards Khafji and sanitising the area around Failaka Island where the US had lost an aircraft. We flew these as pairs, all other tasks being as a dedicated four-ships. Roger Crowder and I were vectored towards two Iraqi Mirages to intercept as part of this tasking but arrived at the scene too late to be effective.

Completing his tour, Mal recalled with humour the events travelling home:

> Junior boys got to fly home in a VC10, the senior boys got to fly back in a Jag. Pete Tholen managed to surge one of his engines over Cairo. He relit it and did not touch it. When he closed the throttle on landing at Coltishall it just seized. So, I got to go to the champagne reception and wave them in.

Flying Officer Mal Rainier standing next to Jaguar XZ119 'Katrina Jane'. (*Courtesy M. Gordon*)

L–R: Flying Officer Nick Collins, Mal Rainer and Flight Lieutenant Dave Foote standing in front of an unknown Jaguar. (*Courtesy M. Rainer*)

We were a pretty open and honest professional bunch. Certainly, compared to other platforms. We weren't dicked about by people who should have backed off and just let them get on with it. In my opinion, the Tornado Force losses were mostly the result of bad luck.

Mal was awarded a DFC for his service during Gulf War 1 and this was recorded in *The London Gazette* on 29 June 1991.

My sincere belief was that, as there had been no burning Spitfires over Dover, there would be no gallantry awards post-conflict. The arrival of a crisp envelope, delivered by the station commander, was something of a shock.

## Flight Lieutenant Michael (Mike) Seares
The following extract has been reproduced with kind permission of the Royal Air Force from an article that the late Group Captain Mike Seares wrote for the 1973–2007 *Jaguar Journal*.

It was 19 January 1991 not the date of the first ever Jaguar operational mission, but my first time, nonetheless. The day before yesterday we had all gone out in a buoyant mood to greet the first 8-ship as they returned, but the smiles were soon wiped from our faces when we realised that 2 of the aircraft had fired their air-to-air missiles and 2 were without their centre line fuel tanks. Had they got involved in some incredible dogfights just off the coast of Kuwait? Beads of sweat were now emerging on our foreheads as we realised that tomorrow we were up for the same thing. They'd survived through, so why shouldn't we? Our mission was led by the then Flight Lieutenant Stevie Thomas; QWI, hard man and just the sort you wanted up the front to instil confidence in us more junior types. We were to attack an SA-2 site in Kuwait KTO, a mad mission if you applied Cold War logic to it as we were going in at medium level and there was no chance of us climbing above the missile engagement envelope. Anticipation and nervous trepidation hung over the brief like a cloud, but now that we were ready it was just a case of wanting to get the job done.

We out briefed with some last-minute intelligence and a pat on the back from the GLO, Pat King, and then wandered out to the aircraft dispersed behind concrete revetments at Muharraq International Airport, our new home in Bahrain. My walk round checks were a little more thorough than usual, and the 4 × 1000lb bombs hanging from the tandem beams on my inboard pylons got a very close inspection. As I strapped in though and started my left to rights it became readily apparent that this jet was very unserviceable and was going nowhere. To cries of 'I just don't believe it' and 'not today of all days', I rushed for the spare cursing the fact that I'd just lost all my extra walk time and was now in a complete rush to make the check in. I briefed the liney to do the externals and make sure all pins were out as I strapped in and fired up as quickly as I could. Just the way you want it on your first operational mission, I don't think. Still, there was no time for worry now and as we taxied out I fully focused on what lay ahead. Stevie called 'Keeper 01 ready take-off' and Air Traffic enquired as to how long we would be away, no answer was the reply for obvious reasons as we got airborne and departed North.

There was rather too much cloud around for my liking, and as I led the back 4 up the transit corridor we went IMC at about 10,000ft. With only the air-to-air TACAN as our friend, in 10 second pairs trail as an 8 ship, this definitely wasn't what we had practised day to day on the work up, but hey this was war, and it would surely get better as we approached the KTO. The word from the front was that we would press to the target area, descend to a minimum of 15,000ft and if we didn't get sight of the ground, RTB. We checked in with the AWACS, were declared 'sweet' and continued in eerie silence towards Kuwait. As we crossed the border into enemy territory I made sure all my weapons switches were live and glued my eyes to the Radar Warning Receiver. 'Time to descend' called Stevie, and down we went, breaking cloud exactly 15,000ft. What were we to do now? How can we do a dive attack if we're not supposed to go below 15,000ft? Well, no time for thoughts like that and as I scanned the ground looking for the familiar circular shape of the SAM 2 site, I incredibly saw one right 2 o'clock at about 8 miles.

Letting Mike Rondot, my wingman know where the target was, I tipped into the attack, releasing my stick of weapons at about 9,000ft, a perilously low height considering the target could shoot back. It was now every man for himself as I became aware of bombs going off north and south of my position and tracer fire everywhere, highlighted by the poor light conditions prevalent below the overcast skies. For some reason I desperately wanted to get back into cloud, in vain hope that it offered me some protection from the forces below. We now had 8 separate Jaguars in cloud, heading as fast as possible towards the safety of the Saudi border, thank God for the big sky theory. As our heart rates slowed, we joined back up for the recovery into Bahrain, laden with the mixed emotions of euphoria at surviving and concern at what we had just done. As the authorisation sheets logged, one aircraft (X) suffered minor flak damage but otherwise no harm done. We, however, were somehow much wiser as to what an operational mission was all about and the kind of dangers we faced, that weren't always attributable to the enemy.

## Flight Lieutenant Edward (Ted) Stringer

Edward deployed on 3 August initially with 6 Squadron, returning six weeks later to the UK to get married in late September.

> This meant I was the first available to go back out again with 41 Squadron. I slotted in, as by this stage I was a pairs leader, I was a first tourist, and junior pilot but I had supervisory capacity so therefore I added some value without clogging up at the top end.

Edward recalled the plan for the RAF Jaguar to go low level during combat and why it was decided to change to medium-level tactics:

> I was part of the planning team, with Stevie Thomas, looking at the low-level stuff. We were looking at how to hit some of these targets, and there was no point in attacking them at low level. He was the QWI and I was just assisting him. We were working out how to conduct pop-up profiles so you could actually hit these targets and penetrate them with dive attacks, therefore using slick bombs

Ted completing his first combat sortie mission on 18 January, piloting Jaguar XZ118 'Buster Gonad', being welcomed home by Flight Lieutenant Alex Emtage. (*Courtesy A. Emtage*)

at high speed. To be honest, finding the targets at low level would be bloody difficult. This is operation certain death! We are going to climb up in full reheat, why would we do this! The QWIs looked at exactly what the Iraqi air defence orbat looked like, and you know the USAF will suppress the Iraq air force. And we were sure this was going to happen. Now, with no air-to-air threat, then the whole charging around at low level hoping to avoid is utterly irrelevant. Instead, you get to the target area and want to find it. Be novel, you can look at a map or a photograph and it all made sense. And every single bomb you throw at it, you will do a dive attack, which is nice and stable. And you will throw high-speed bombs at it, so if it's a hard target, or anything else, you will hit it. Why would you now drop yourself down to the one thing the Iraqis absolutely had superiority on? Was it 400 AAA pieces at just one airfield!

Sensible decisions were made to fly medium level before starting the conflict and agreed by the command team of the Jaguar force. Edward believes they were influenced by the experience and talented manner of his colleagues that had completed the intensive Jaguar RAF Qualified Weapons Instructors course.

The Jaguar weapons instructors course was really professional. The course taught a Jaguar pilot to really understand the weapons systems and the weapons coming online. Spending time with industry, how not just the weapon and the bombs works, but the aeroplane works as well. So, when CRV-7 came in we absolutely knew how to aim and fire it. More importantly, the 960 fuse, which came in at the start of the conflict. We understood it and never had a problem with it. This was because Mike Gordon asked all the right questions and set the conditions, and beneath were the QWIs, Frog Tholen and Stevie Thomas. They utterly knew the weapons, they had been to Marconi, so they knew how to put all the zeros and ones in, an example, so you got the maximum ten-second delay when you release before armed.

On 20 January Edward flew Jaguar XZ106 'Rule Britannia' as part of a four-ship, call sign Keeper 01. This was his third combat sortie:

We were airborne, target out in fog over Kuwait, went back to Bahrain. As we had been getting airborne, Frog Tholen said, 'Should we be getting airborne?' The Victor had got airborne and had almost gone out into its own weather system. As it rotated, the vapour coming off the wings in the temperature, Frog turned around and said, 'Look where the dew point and temperature are going to cross over and only a degree apart. And sure enough we went out in fog. We diverted to Dhahran. A total bomb burst. I think there were eight aircraft coming from four

Flight Lieutenant Edward Stringer seated in a Jaguar, possibly XZ106 'Rule Britannia'. Note the AIM-9L Sidewinder on the bomb tally paintwork, and the painted message on the 1,000lb bomb on the starboard wing underside pylon. (*Courtesy A. Emtage*)

> different points of the compass, and we are all very low on petrol. We totally lost each other and bizarrely we all landed on the runway all under fuel minimum. We were all trying to land on an instrument landing, speaking to Saudi air traffic. Day four of the war, no petrol. I would not have been surprised if someone banged out or simply ran out of petrol. But all of us managed to taxi in this almost perfect formation and taxied off the runway.

On 22 January, he was flying Jaguar XZ367 'White Rose', with Flying Officer Nick Collins as his No. 2 in Jaguar XZ118 'Buster Gonad', conducting a CSAR sortie. They were with two other aircraft on a similar task. The four aircraft claimed the longest combat sortie of any Jaguar formation during Gulf War 1, totalling five hours' flying time:

> I remember getting Nick up to a Victor tanker with about 700kg of fuel left on board on that one and doing a low-level pass very close to Iranian coastal waters as we wanted to investigate a fast patrol ship and wanted to see if it was an Iranian flag on the back! We kept getting vectored onto things that weren't that well understood. There was a lot of tanking and going back to a Victor and try and find it in the middle of nowhere and wait for Nick to plug

in. I think there was no way we could go and land and we had to get into the tanker, we are refuelling, or we are not. We both got in and carried on with the mission.

On 5 February, flying Jaguar XX962, 'Fat Slags', Edward was part of a nine-ship formation that was tasked to bomb and destroy a communications site consisting of a relay building and radio mast. The formation dropped four 1,000lb bombs with 952 fuses fitted:

> Still standing, almost certainly. It doesn't mean that any of the aerials were working on it. The fuse would have gone off on the ground, from memory 5 or 10m. You aim at the mast and one of the bombs will go bang and close to the top of the mast and therefore take out the aerial, or slice through the cables. You won't drop the mast. You are going to be really fortunate to drop a slick bomb from 30,000ft and 8 miles away and it happens to hit the base of the mast.

Edward commented on the performance of the Jaguar and his conclusions on the Gulf War.

> It suits all aeroplanes to be warm and dry, it's when it is cold damp and brittle that it breaks them. The Jaguar was working in Oman for a long time. The Adour was always a reliable engine, it did not produce much thrust. As long as you did not overcook the first-generation nav kit, when it worked, it worked really well. It was just a right mix of being sophisticated enough to do that job, but simple enough you weren't nursing an overheated diva around the sky. Apart from the odd single-engine landing, which I did a couple. It remained remarkably serviceable as an airframe. That was under Mick Cartwright and a group of engineers that worked really well together.
> The first lesson that comes out the Gulf, the Jaguar force accidently lucked in, because the air force rushed what was believed to be the A team out first off. By the A team, what was meant, was the top end of the pilot element. It took 6 Squadron, a core squadron, out to Oman. Why did we think this would work? This was like picking your football team based on the salaries you are paying. It might work, rather than who plays best on the pitch! You could end up with no goalkeeper and eleven strikers and wonder why it does not work. And that is what happened! It took some grown-up mature characters to realise they might have the most senior squadron leader there, and the XO from their own squadron. Actually, they had no real function other than to be line pilots. And that does not work. And one

Flight Lieutenant Edward Stringer next to Jaguar XZ364 'Saddam' after returning from a mission. (*Courtesy 41 Sqn, RAF*)

Flight Lieutenant Edward Stringer being interviewed by the world media. (*Courtesy S. Young*)

lesson that has followed me around my whole career was, don't rush your home team out the door!

Bill Pixton gave some real thought to the 'team of teams'. Who do you put together in the various four-ships. He tried to think about it. If you are going to spend a lot of time together, are they going to get along together? So, let's put four people in who are not going to be at each other's throats. I know there was one four-ship that got along really well. They were put together but were so opposite. But they really gelled.

The squadron could make sensible decisions, if you end up with a totally heavy outfit I would argue it happened to the Tornado force a bit. Bill Pixton was able to sit there as a squadron leader and work all this and he worked out what he wanted to do with his squadron, not part of a machine. It meant he could break with convention. And that does not mean he can be unconventional as this causes baggage. I would argue to do the right thing in these circumstances, what you assess to be the right thing. Even if that is not usual.

The Jaguar force are a very interesting mix of people, laid back on the ground and very professional in the air. It's a mix, a mongrel force. Some of the people that are crossover, some of these people had time on the Canberra. And then the youngsters who come through flying training and at the top of their game and went to Jaguar. You have now got a mixture of old, bold, other forces and some of the brightest youngsters who had come through the air force flying training system.

Pilots' Personal Extracts 117

Flight Lieutenant Edward Stinger.
(*Courtesy W. Pixton and M. Rainier*)

## Flight Lieutenant Pete (Frog) Tholen

> I was nicknamed Frog because of having bow legs. At officer training, to do squat thrusts it was more comfortable for me to put my legs outside of my arms rather than the traditional inside and fair enough it did end up making me look rather frog like.

Before the Gulf War Pete was on a ground tour based at RAF Upavon in a staff position in charge of booking aircraft range slots. It was a very boring repetitive post but had the advantage of allowing freedom to be out of the office providing my primary task was completed. This allowed me to go and visit some mates, including one at RAF Brawdy in south Wales, initially just to have a couple of days flying in the back seat of the Hawk. As it happened I managed to get requalified on the Hawk very quickly:

> I was in the bar at Brawdy and a chap called Chalky White said he needed a pilot to tow a 2 v 1 (an air combat exercise). I jokingly said, 'I'll do that for you.' to which he replied, 'I wish you could!' The station commander – who was stood behind us – said, 'Why not? go to the Sim, I will do a weather check with you tomorrow morning to check you out and off you go!'. The station commander was a fantastic character, I am not sure it could happen these days!

Pete remembers the start of the Gulf War:

> I got dragged back to Upavon from Brawdy. I then got put into Strike Command for about a week. One of the jobs I got given while there was to work out an R&R plan for the Jaguar guys that had gone out on the initial detachment. I worked out that the Jaguar QWIs left in the UK were myself and Steve Thomas. I went to see my group captain, Doug McGregor, and said, 'Right I think I need to go and get requalified on the Jaguar, because it looks like I will be going out.'
> He said, 'You will never, ever go to Bahrain.'
> I think it was seven days later that I sent him a postcard from Bahrain. It was slightly odd initially as I wasn't actually on a squadron at the time, I joined the group quite late. I knew everybody, as the Jag force and RAF Coltishall is quite a small place.
> So, I went back to RAF Coltishall and before I deployed I had to do two or three trips, including a tanking trip. I then took my wife to Paris for two days, then went straight out to Bahrain with Bill Pixton and Strike Gordon. We had a four-hour handover with the QWIs already out there, Alex Musket being one of them. We got shown the plans that had been drawn up so far, and then they left!

He remembers with humour:

> I was slightly annoyed as everyone had the chance to increase their life insurance. I wasn't allowed to increase it because I was deemed to be disloyal as I was leaving the service. I was not too bothered because I was out there doing my job with a bunch of mates. However, it really annoyed the wife!

On arrival pilots got put into their composite four-ships and Pete recalls how Wing Commander Bill Pixton made his command decisions:

> One great example of Bill's leadership was, while he was always the commander, he would always seek opinions of others and looked at the pros and cons of everything before making that decision. When the decision was made it was always stated very clearly, 'This is what we are doing', but you always felt your voice had been listened to.
>
> One of the first training trips we did with Bill, we were planning it out, a low-level route. I think it was an eight-ship. We were to wiz round a local route, come back to Bahrain. I was No. 2 and I said to Bill. 'You know this trip is slightly too long with that fuel?'
>
> His reply, 'Yep, they are responsible for their own aircraft and need to realise that from here on in, not the flight lead of the formation. It is big boy rules!'
>
> We also talked about fuel reserves when tanking, should we have enough fuel when behind the tanker to divert just in case we were unsuccessful getting fuel for whatever reason. His response was the same, 'The rules are there, but what you do in your aircraft is up to you.' I seem to recall there were several occasions ending up behind the tanker with very little fuel . . . it definitely sharpened up the refuelling technique!
>
> Bill made it very clear from the start it was not peacetime and there was flexibility in the rules if you could justify your actions. Which was great because it meant everyone could concentrate on the important stuff.
>
> He was directly backed up incredibly well by two people. Mike Gordon, with his style of leadership, made sure we all knew exactly how Bill wanted it done. He also had Bill's ear. If Mike ever saw something and thought it was not a good idea he was assertive enough to make sure that the subject was raised and addressed.
>
> The second was Mick Cartwright, the engineering warrant officer. I remember we were on the morning-to-afternoon shift and I asked Mr Cartwright for cluster bombs throughout on this particular mission. When we got the target and looked at it we realised we had the wrong weapon selection. I rang up Mick and said, 'Can you rearm the aeroplanes?'
>
> 'How many?' he replied.
>
> 'All of them!'

He just went, 'Yep alright.'

If you'd done that on a normal peacetime squadron he would just have said 'no'. Anybody would have said no!!! It was an enormous task which would require serious team effort. But the guys did it and not once did they complain. He never gave the impression that anybody was rushing, overworked. Everything was doable. Before our first trip he popped up the ladder and said, 'I will see you when you get back.' His leadership was just outstanding.

Bill, for the first two weeks, was very keen that we should learn any lessons from the days events, so every night he would have the entire contingent of pilots in his room. He would turn around and say, 'Well what have we learned today?' He was determined that no one would be put in jeopardy due to lack of communication. Everyone had an equal voice and that is why we ended up doing 'random timing' tactics. As an example, people would say they were getting a little wary down the back. Hence we varied the distance between aircraft, eventually making it random. All types of attack profiles to make them less predictable.

On 18 January Pete took part in his first combat mission, flying Jaguar XX748 as part of a four-ship formation with call sign Bowler 51 flight. The lead was Wing Commander Bill Pixton, with Flight Lieutenant Ted Stringer and Flying Officer Nick Collins in the formation. They were tasked to support a USAF A-10 FAC.

It was bizarre, enroute we contacted the control agency and asked what is the cloud base? We flew with this card on our kneepad and there is a code on there, which gave the actual cloudbase. They gave us the number and it was 4,000ft. So down we go in Tactical formation. (2 pairs in close formation separated longitudinally). Passing about 2,000ft, we are still in close formation as we are still in thick cloud. The A-10 saying, 'Come on guys help me out, I am getting shot at here.' I was thinking, 'If he is worried about being shot at, this is not good!' He then says he is pulling off target due to intense fire. Not only have we got heavily loaded aircraft, I have very little fuel left. We started to pull up and I thought, 'Right, I am going to jettison these bombs live as I know there is enemy below me.' … Not a good idea. That is when this AAA went between Bill and me. (We are still in close formation!) It exploded close to Bill, in quite a dramatic fashion. For some reason I say, 'triple A', (remember I had never seen AAA before.) We part company in cloud, clueless as to what we are doing really, we are at the wrong speed, we stagger up back through the cloud and we do not see each other again until we get on the ground.

Pete was one of the first pilots to fire the CRV-7 rockets from the Jaguar:

We got these weapons, and Bill Pixton was laughing as he said to me and Stevie, 'You better work out the gravity drop of these things.' (When you go through the

*Above left, above right and right*: Flight Lieutenant Pete Tholen returns from his first combat mission flying Jaguar XX748 on 18 January. (*Courtesy P. Tholen*)

QWI course you spend a lot of time doing maths fully believing that it is theory only, never to be repeated.) We gave it our best shot, went off to the range, fired at the targets and thought, yep that seems to work. Unfortunately, when I first fired mine in anger it was when we were on CSAR mission and it was at a boat that we thought had SAM-8s on board. I was mooching across the sea as low as I dare. I see a boat and put my manually calculated aiming symbol on the target. Then one pod of rockets, nineteen, went straight into the sea almost immediately in front of me. I pull up going, 'Holy shit,' then I think, 'Oh my God, they have SAM-8s, I better push down again to get low.' Then I thought, 'Now I am going to hit the sea and pull up again.' This boat with the Iraqis on board must have thought, 'How can we lose, they are a bunch of buffoons yo-yoing towards us.' It was not my finest hour.

On 30 January Pete was flying as No. 2 piloting Jaguar XZ356 'Mary Rose' as part of Longstop flight with Wing Commander Bill Pixton flying XZ364 'Saddam'. They were conducting an attack against a Polish-designed Polnocny C-class landing ship that was transiting near the mouth of the Shatt al-Arab waterway.

We had the weapon aiming sorted by now. To be honest, we never really talked through how to attack a boat. We aimed where the weakest point was, the deck. Because these rockets were so accurate, because they are doing Mach 4! They all went slightly high. If you are aiming at the deck and in a shallow descent and aim slightly high it means you are going to miss the boat. If we had thought

Waiting to taxi and enjoying the sunshine with the canopy up. The Jaguar canopy was legacy in design and manually operated, not like the Tornado, which was hydraulically locked. Pete Tholen recalled it was just bliss in that heat! (*Courtesy P. Tholen*)

about it a wee bit more and aimed at the waterline they might have gone short but ricocheted into the ship's side. This is where I swore, the video clip of which, they showed on TV thinking that I had said 'got it'. I hadn't! We were so annoyed with ourselves for missing with the rockets. It was a misty day and we couldn't see each other. We basically set up an academic range pattern and were calling things like 'downwind' so we knew where we were. Out of sheer bloody frustration we strafed this ship as many times as we could, with HE.

As much as I would like to cover myself in blazes of glory, we were fairly certain the sailors had already abandoned ship.

Another weapon limitation that Pete recalls about the Jaguar force during the conflict is the fact they were not experts at the medium-level, 'dive-bombing', weapon release profiles. The Jaguar had always traditionally delivered weapons at low level:

We had never envisaged doing this high-angle dive-bombing-type run; we never thought about the lag between the weaponeering symbol and the release. This definitely caught a few of us out. It was very easy to think that the weapon had failed to release automatically (and so used the manual function) actually they had not got to that point in the sky where the bombs release automatically.

One CSAR event that occurred in the early stages of the conflict was when Pete was flying on a mission and heard on his radio a USAF F-16 that was in trouble:

One of the first times we went into Iraq, from the west, with a barrel load of other aeroplanes. This F-16 came up on frequency and said, 'Hey guys, I have got a slight problem. My throttle is not working.' We did not pay much attention to him until he later informed us, 'It's not my throttle, it's my engine that is not working!' He glided out over the sea and ejected. Because it took him so long to glide to the water, when he ejected he was picked up very quickly.

At the time of the Gulf War the UK was not looking at exporting the Jaguar aircraft. It is interesting to note Pete's comments on how this aircraft conducted its operations:

There was no political constraints at that time to make sure the Jaguar was seen to be doing the job that was advertised. And all the commanders cared about was, did we launch, and did we get to the target? About two weeks into the conflict they started to get worried about collateral. It was then, how were we identifying the targets, how could we be absolutely certain what we thought was the target definitely was?

Performance wise the Jaguar was poor, let's face it. I remember, not deliberately, we blew a BBC cameraman off his Land-Rover at the end of the runway! (Not the

L–R: Wing Commander Bill Pixton, Flight Lieutenants Pete Tholen, Edward Stringer and Flying Officer Nick Collins standing beside Jaguar XZ106 'Johnny Fartpants'. (*Courtesy P. Tholen*)

brightest place to set up and film departing aircraft.) When we were asked why we did not go higher over him we turned around and said, that was the best take-off performance we could manage, we were at max thrust! If an engine failed on take-off you would have to eject, you would have no other choice.

To reach the best altitude for weapon delivery we were climbing pretty much full thrust all the way from take-off, so you could argue that performance was core!

On one occasion myself and Bill got vectored onto a couple of Mirage aircraft. I was leading and said to the control agency, 'You do realise what we are, don't you?'

He said, 'You have got Sidewinders haven't you?'

So off we went. I don't recall going that far north but it was an interesting few minutes! In a dogfight the Jaguar would need most of Wales to turn around in. The good side of the Jaguar was its reliability, it was awesome. I can't remember anyone not getting airborne from a technical malfunction. The weapon aiming (once we received and installed it) combined with the head-up display symbology for the CRV-7 meant the ease of aiming was incredible! But you would run out of rockets quickly. We also carried CBU-87, a horrible weapon (as it is a cluster bomb) but, a very effective weapon, and you don't need a highly accurate weapon-aiming solution for it. At the end of January we were running out of fuses. Being one of the weapon reps for the Jaguar, a meeting was held and I ventured the opinion 'If it helps, the Jaguar force is quite happy to go with any fuse.' I had already spoken to the Tornados' weapons guy, and told him, 'You are doing bridges, you need a weapon with a funky fuse,' whereas we were hitting targets on the ground. There was a gentlemen's agreement between us and the Tornado boys that they should have first choice. The Jaguar meanwhile were looking at World War Two vintage fusing but that was all we needed. The check on the fuse was to wind the little windmill on the front and if you could continue to wind it up, you ran away as the bomb was now armed!

With the standard 1,000lb bomb I don't think we hit much. The weapon where we did most of the damage was the CRV-7. The laser rangefinder worked well and when stabilised in the dive, we were getting very accurate ranging. The Jaguar was not like some other aircraft where you have to watch your trim, she was an easy aeroplane to fly. Once the pipper was on the target and you had a laser range lock, when you pulled the trigger you were pretty much guaranteed that nineteen or thirty-eight rockets would go through whatever you were aiming at. We achieved a lot of good results with this particular weapon.

*Right and below*: Jaguars taking on fuel from a Victor tanker high above the desert. (*Courtesy P. Tholen*)

*Above and left*: Flight Lieutenant Pete Tholen preparing for a mission. (*Courtesy P. Tholen*)

Pilots' Personal Extracts   127

The EW kit we had on the aircraft at the time was very good! Not particularly well programmed when we first arrived but once sorted out we got a good return of information.

We all liked carrying the Sidewinders, but it was a bit of a safety blanket. Nobody could turn around and say it ruined the Jaguar's performance, because the Jaguar didn't turn anyway!

Pete has fond memories of his time in the Gulf and of the return home:

It was a bunch of blokes who all got along really well, flying aeroplanes, and did what they were trained to do. There was all sorts of buffoonery that went on. But that is what made it fun to be honest. It was a very unhealthy lifestyle, we were staying in a lovely hotel, with a great bar. There was a fantastic band, a Filipino tribute band, in the bar downstairs in the Diplomat. The first time a Scud alarm went off they had no idea what to do, nor did the public, who ran off. So, we were left in this huge bar with this band and they looked at us. We turned around to them and said, 'Play on!' There was people putting these jay cloths over their faces thinking it would protect them from gas attack, they were just wasting their time and we said, 'Just sit back and enjoy yourself!'

Flight Lieutenant Pete Tholen arriving back at RAF Coltishall on 13 March 1991 flying Jaguar XZ119 'Katrina Jane'. It was written in the squadron diary, 'Frog – Surge Drill, Pah! Who says you can't tank on one engine! (*Courtesy 41 Sqn, RAF*)

On the 'leopard trail' back to the UK Pete had an engine surge flying Jaguar XZ119 'Katrina Jane'. He recalled with humour:

> I think it was around the first tanking bracket, we had not even got to Saudi yet, and there was a little bit of a fart from one of the engines! I thought, 'I am not touching that engine again.' I left it, including for the fly-by. I was quite pleased actually, a fixed thrust (on one-engine) formation fly-by! When I landed and shut the engines down it should take about a minute for the blades to stop turning… on that occasion, I think it was three seconds! When we got back to Coltishall and having completed the fly-past, we landed and climbed out of the aeroplanes. We were mingin', we had been in these aeroplanes for six or seven hours, but it was all smiles and beer as we were back home. I turned around and was met by a High Ranking Air Officer, whose name I very rudely cannot remember. As I start to salute, he said, 'No, I salute you.' I thought, 'What a magnificent thing to do.'

## Flight Lieutenant Stephen (Stevie) Thomas

On the outbreak of hostilities, Stevie was teaching at 226 OCU Squadron based at RAF Lossiemouth. He was an experienced pilot, previously serving with 54 Squadron from 1985 to 1988 then moving to Lossiemouth in 1989 as a QWI, posted into STANEVAL weapons. He remembers Gulf War events unfolding:

> It was through the news like everyone else, chatting to mates at Coltishall. One of my buddies down there saying, 'Things are turning pink down here at the moment.'

This referred to the pink paint colour scheme being adopted on the Jaguar aircraft and aircraft preparing to deploy. Stevie continued with training but due to the lack of QWIs he was aware he might get called to deploy on operations:

> Not knowing, nobody did, either political or otherwise. We just got on with the day job. We were not planning to get involved, but if people were going from Colt they may be needing to borrow someone from the OCU. I ended up going out as part of the roulement in November. Pete Tholen and I took over from two QWIs who were coming back. At the time I was conducting my A2 QFI, on my second sortie in a T-Bird. It was a trip to Colt to qualify me and drop me off to get a flight out to Bahrain.

The role of the QWI was to assist with planning and delivery of weapons and tactics, enhancing these skills among the deployed Jaguar pilots:

> When I pitched up, all the training was low level over the desert as that's all we knew. At some point, and it was cutting it fine, it was clear that the routing we

would have to take to get us in and out of Iraq was medium level. The throwaway comment was that if we want to deliver low we would have to go through Jane's World of SAMs, MANPADs and AAAs to get to the target, to then climb back up through Jane's World just to get back to a safe routing. So why don't we accept the fact that we were going to be at medium level, steep dive deliveries. That was the general conversation between the QWI element, flight commanders and the boss. The weapon was one aspect and the delivery profile the other.

On the day it all kicked off, my phone rings in the hotel. It's Baggers, 'We're on Steve.' Downstairs somebody was para phrasing a quote from Blackadder, 'Well we brief at 10 o'clock, airborne for half ten and dead by ten to eleven.' Great humour.

This was the first time the RAF was taking part in an operation where there was a high degree of hostile surface threats and careful consideration had to be made for planning against these types of targets:

I remember when planning for a certain mission there was some knowledge of an SA-8 near to the target. There was a lot of attention being paid to this threat, quite rightly it was there! Subsequently I recall, there we were collectively

Flight Lieutenant Stevie Thomas in the cockpit of Jaguar XZ118 'Buster Gonad' ready to launch on his first combat mission on 17 January. (*Courtesy S. Thomas*)

worrying about one SA-8 and the real int with these things dotted all over the place. I remember taking a picture of the int map one day, you could just make the outline of Kuwait because there were all these dots of these systems everywhere. We did not even have intelligence that the Iraqi air force had bugged off. It became obvious quite quickly, however, that they weren't there.

Frog and I were the first to test the new CRV-7 2.75 rockets from the Jaguar. Stevie recalls this occasion in detail:

The rockets were a good addition; I remember the rockets arriving and Frog and I would go and give them a go. Initially, we had extremely limited data on the rockets, apart from anything that leaves the pod at Mach 3 is unlikely to have much gravity drop. In regard to symbology, we did not get this for some time from back home. Often we would talk to people who had experience using them. So, we were delivering them in revisionary mode. Cranking up an appropriate mileage in the HUD and the calculations we worked out, they worked. It's a relatively short distance anyway, 3 miles into a mile. Us able to fire anything out of that was a long way. I had a fellow QWI buddy down in Oman, he reckoned a certain mileage will work, therefore go for a cooking range of whatever we said. Initially using them in an academic profile and I seem to recall the war pod had nineteen rockets and the training pod had half a dozen. We would fire these in a single shot with a training pod. Then came the opportunity to fire the war pods. We flipped a coin between Frog and I who was going to fly with them. I won, two pods of nineteen rockets, all dispatched within 760 milliseconds I recall. My words on my cockpit voice was 'Fuck my old boots.' On return on the debrief people kept playing it on replay. It was quite impressive to see those things come out. Frog was flying line astern to video the rockets through his HUD, the rockets came out. When we were making our way back to Muharraq it seemed he had ingested some of the shit from the rockets into one of his intakes.

Stevie recalls flying on a combat mission:

We weren't entirely certain on our range, with the drop tanks on and bombs on the centre line. Subsequent missions we thought, 'Hang on we must have fuel', so fuel tanks on the centre line and bombs on the inline. Anybody who turns around and says they weren't frightened was lying. One trip we were in CAP, just going around in circles. We would get told via C2 if anything was coming out heading towards the coast. I got locked up by some chappie on the coast who had an interest in us. I was turning away, and he showed

Qualified Weapon Instructors Flight Lieutenant Pete Tholen and Steve Thomas preparing to go to the range to test CRV-7 rockets. (*Courtesy P. Tholen*)

interest in us again, the next thing I noticed was something smoking high speed. 'Fuck me, he's shifting.' Thinking it was a contrail or something. Hang on a minute, that's not an aircraft, it continued to smoke down the hill. The smoke stopped, and all the lights went out. It was obviously one of those US Weasels.

CRV-7 2.75in rocket pod fitted to an underside starboard Jaguar wing. (*Courtesy 41 Sqn, RAF*)

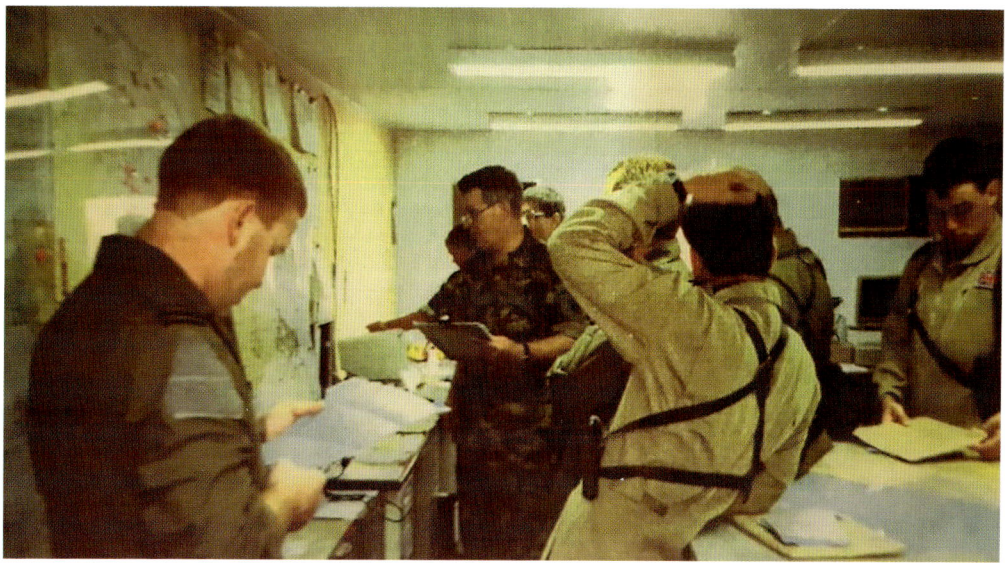

L–R: Flight Lieutenant Stevie Thomas, Mike Seares, back and arm to head, Major Pat King, and Flying Officer Mal Rainier. Recorded in the unofficial squadron diary as, '05.50Hrs, brief said Demi-Gods with vital int, never cease to be amazed at how warriors fall asleep, read Blueys, open parcels and listen intently to the GLO at the same time.' (*Courtesy M. Rainier*)

Flight Lieutenant Stevie Thomas heading down to the flight line. (*Courtesy M. Rainier*)

One mission, I was leading on this occasion, it was an SA-2 site. We were in cloud for quite a lot of the way. I said to the guys we would not go below a certain height as part of the brief. We get to a height nominated, tip in, acquire the target. We went down a couple of times at height to clear it coming out of cloud about thirty seconds from the target. We got in, and got out. Parking back up at Bahrain, Hoppy said, 'Stevie T, you lied to me, you did.' With a big smile on his face. 'We weren't going to go low, lying bastard.' We hit the target though.

*Left and below*: Flight Lieutenant Stevie Thomas landing back at RAF Coltishall on 13 March 1991, flying Jaguar XZ118 'Buster Gonad'. (*Courtesy M. Rainer*)

Reflecting on the Gulf War, Stevie remembers his colleagues:

> We had a good team of people; an excellent boss and I wouldn't have missed it for the world.

For his service he was Mentioned in Dispatches and gazetted on 29 June 1991.

## Flight Lieutenant Simon Young

Simon recalls receiving the news that he was to deploy on operations and a close call on his way to Bahrain:

> I remember my boss Tim Hewlett coming to our house to tell us the news – my wife opened the door – which made things a bit tricky as she knew immediately what he was going to say. I remember being torn between feeling both exhilaration and a strong feeling of guilt for how I knew Margaret would be taking it. Toby Craig, Dick MacCormac and I were to be deployed out to reinforce the pilots just about to start operations.
>
> One of the scariest times for me out of the whole thing was when we deployed out. Me, Toby and Dick flew out to Bahrain in the back of a Herc and initially landed at Riyadh. We went out with fairly minimal kit, expecting to get most of our kit out there. We had a gas mask each. If I am honest we were pretty blasé about the whole NBC threat. The Jag force did not really have a real NBC capability like the Tornado had so there wasn't much point. I remember when we arrived – the entire airport terminal had been turned into a huge hospital to cope with the huge, expected ground offensive casualties – it was full of nurses, doctors etc who were desperate for news of what was happening. We told them what we could, which wasn't much, and gave them some recent newspapers, which they seemed grateful for.
>
> Shortly after this, Riyadh came under a Scud attack. All the sirens went off, you heard the Patriot missiles going off and intercepting the Scud missiles overhead – the reality of the war hit us all at that point! We were rapidly led down to makeshift shelters (store rooms). I remember looking at Dick and Toby, who had their gas masks on, and thinking, 'My God, what is happening here!' Most people were in their NBC suits, we managed to get some off a shelf and we popped them on quickly. I remember this chap turning up in his jacket and tie and he stood in the middle of the shelter with the attack warning sirens blaring. All twenty of us in NBC suits just stared at him like you would a canary in a mine! It was really surreal. Once the all clear rang out we quickly made the decision to do whatever was needed to get out of this place. I remember finding the movers and talking us onto the next flight out. A couple of hours later we

got on a night flight Herc schedule en route Bahrain. As the aircraft took off, we flew straight into another Scud attack. I remember seeing the Patriot missiles leaving their launchers from one of the Herc windows and hearing the explosions around us as the Scud warheads were intercepted – it was quite terrifying and unlike being shot at in a Jaguar, where at least you had some control over your destiny. I recall feeling helpless and for me it was the most vulnerable I felt for the entire war.

When we arrived in Bahrain there was no time to dwell on what had just happened. We were met by the boss, and informed that we were on the morning bombing wave. Dick and Toby had flown from Bahrain before and were aware of the basic procedures. I hadn't so I must admit to being a tad flustered at this point, but we all grabbed some sleeping pills to fight off the jet lag and got back to the hotel to get some rest before going sausage side the next day.

Simon's first sortie was on 23 January, flying Jaguar XZ119 'Katrina Jane' as part of Keeper flight, an eight-ship. The target was an Iraqi AAA position.

The Jaguar force experienced many SAM launchers in close proximity to aircraft and formations, however, Simon is believed to be one of the only Jaguar pilots who had a direct launch of a SAM against him during a combat mission. On 31 January, flying in Jaguar XZ356 'Mary Rose', he was conducting SUCAP duties with Squadron Leader Dick Midwinter as his No. 2. The story is taken up having checked in with the control agency:

Dick and I were capping overhead the USS Missouri, that itself was an amazing experience. When it fired its 15 inch guns the whole ship would rock backwards in the water. I remember thinking I wouldn't want to be on the end of that barrage! We were carrying BL755s cluster munitions, and if we got tasked them, then we would have to go in at low level to release them! There was a report of a convoy going down the main Kuwait coast road. We were tasked to go and have a look at it. I was leading the pair at the time. At that point I lost Dick on the switchover of the freqs. I was getting all the briefing but Dick couldn't hear it. We circled for a bit above AAA altitude I tried to get him back up on the radio. Basically one of us would stay above and watch, while the other attacked and vice versa. I had to brief the low-level attack we were going to do on the hoof! The convoy we had been tasked to look at must have been hit by something else or just wasn't there. However, on the road we could see trucks and because they didn't want to be targeted there was a lot of distance between each of them, I guess a minute or two between each truck so they didn't appear in a big convoy. I saw one of these soft-skinned trucks and

I decided to attack it. Dick stayed up and gave top cover and I selected one CBU and attacked in a pretty steep dive. Because of this I'd be quite high at release, so I figured I would have to release the bombs well ahead of the truck to give the bomblets time to float down on their parachutes, so I released at about 1,500ft. As I pulled off I rolled onto my back and could see the bomblets starting to go off just short of the truck I thought, 'Shit I've missed.' Then one of the very last bomblets dropped on the back of this truck and it veered off into a ditch on fire – I think I saw the driver jump out. Out the corner of my eye I saw what I thought was a ZSU and called it to Dick. He came down and had a go and missed. Then I made another attack targeting it again, dropping the remaining CBU from a reasonable height! As I was pulling off Dick called 'missile'. I think it was a hand-held missile. At that point I flared and broke left and I remember thinking, 'I am not turning very fast', so I then punched everything off the aircraft and carried on with the break, I saw the missile go up on the right-hand side of me. It didn't lock and just shot upwards. It was a great call by Dick, as I didn't see it immediately – it probably saved my bacon. We had a few beers in the bar that night.

A destroyed Iraqi Army ZSU-345 'Shilka' self-propelled anti-aircraft gun (SPAAG), similar to what Squadron Leader Dick Midwinter and Flight Lieutenant Simon Young engaged during a combat mission on 31 January. (*Courtesy milfactory.com*)

Simon continued to recall his combat experience. On the morning of 1 February, again flying as part of an eight-ship, Jaguars were tasked to attack al-Jaber airfield, Kuwait, which was being used by the Iraqi air force.

> I do vaguely remember that mission. We were going for the airfield infrastructure that day and I remember missing the specified target. There was a lot of AAA.
>
> Generally we targeted mobile artillery a lot and I also remember attacking the Silkworm site on the coast. This was with VT 1,000-pounders, I remember a number of Toby's and Dick's bombs going off directly overhead the target (we often spotted each other's bombs).
>
> The squadron would try to get reconnaissance pictures of the mobile artillery targets we had attacked. What the Iraqis would do was often leave the damaged artillery and APCs there and take away the serviceable ones, because they knew we knew where they were. You would then know the ones you had hit the day before!

An artist's impression of Flight Lieutenant Simon Young flying Jaguar XZ367 'Debbie' on 1 February attacking al-Jaber airfield. (*Source unknown*)

Aerial photograph taken by a US aircraft in July 1992, showing bomb damage to one of the hardened aircraft shelters at al-Jaber. (*Courtesy Global security.org*)

Commenting on the Jaguar's performance in combat, Simon said:

> I loved the Jaguar. It had its performance issues, but it was reliable, and a stable weapons platform and all of the kit we had worked. We were supported very well by the boffins, all the time updates would come in, stuff would improve. They would sort out ballistics on this and that. Weapon aiming got a lot sharper as you got into the war. The aircraft held up really well, we were operating often at the extremes of the release to service, certainly in Oman, and at high temperatures. A lot of the other fighters with high-tolerance engines suffered sand damage during the war operations but the Jaguar engine didn't generate a great deal of thrust anyway and it didn't seem to make any difference! The ground crew were fantastic, too. We always felt well supported and looked after and rarely suffered any unserviceability.

Simon remembered how difficult it was to speak to family back home with a limited amount of modern communications.

> You tried to call back as much as you could. It was quite stressful for the families back home. I knew my boss back at 54 Squadron was on the phone to my wife every day to tell her I had landed safely – he was great that way and I know it made a big difference to Margaret.

*Above*: Flight Lieutenant Simon Young conducting pre-checks around his aircraft before a mission. (*Courtesy S. Young*)

*Left and opposite*: Flight Lieutenant Simon Young in Jaguar XZ367 'White Rose'. (*Courtesy S. Young*)

Pilots' Personal Extracts 141

*Chapter 5*

# Squadron Ground Crew

> On one particular sortie I was going down the dive, something distracted me, I think the RWR. I committed and pickled. The guard of the stick caught the top of the pickle button and it slammed shut and nothing came off the aeroplane! I was so annoyed with this, I snapped it off. When I got on the ground I said to the Warrant, 'I want all those guards removed.' 'OK sir, they're your aeroplanes.' He went around and snapped them all off!
>
> Wing Commander Bill Pixton

Warrant Officer Mick Cartwright was the squadron engineering warrant officer. His role was to oversee all maintenance and serviceability of the Jaguar fleet throughout the roulemont. The following is his personal account of the conflict:

> The first sign of trouble in the Gulf came during RAM 90. There we were, comfortably installed at Bergstrom AFB, Texas, while 'the best of the best' pitched their recce skills against the Americans and Australians. When the news came through I came back to Coltishall via Gander, night stop, engine change on Herc. And then onto Lyneham, followed by a bumpy ride back to Coltishall in a minibus. The guys had a successful competition, returning with a couple of trophies.
>
> I was told that 6 Squadron had left, taking a number of my key personnel: engine and radar trade managers Ian Nelson and Pete Lean, and, of course, numerous recce guys. Their period of deployment was assumed to be three months. The question was, who would go next? I had a meeting with the boss on 13 August and started to put my case for 41 to replace 6, highlighting the fact that we were the most prepared, having been successfully tacevaled twice in a year. At this point he put up his hand and said we were going anyway, probably in November. In the meantime, we had to set up a training programme to cover all possible conditions we were likely to encounter out there.
>
> September 1990, of course, also involved 41 and 54 Squadrons in the 50th Anniversary of the Battle of Britain, which meant that, along with Flying Officer Tom Barratt, Barry Todd, Trev Hollett and young Darren Reynolds, I was sent to Uxbridge for a week's colour party training with the Queen's Colour Squadron. On the day everything went off well and the flypast, led by the boss, was superb. I will ever forget

# Squadron Ground Crew 143

*Above and below*: The first photo first shows Jaguars with canopy protective covers fitted to the front of the aircraft. The second shows ground crew working in the avionics bays. (*Courtesy M. Cartwright*)

the pride we felt, standing there behind the squadron standards, and being reviewed by the Queen.

There followed lots of training and lots of leave, and our departure date was given as 26 November, a typical balmy Norfolk day. My manpower was set at around 200 men, but I wasn't allowed to pick who I wanted from 54. 'Don't worry about it', I was told. 'You won't go short.' After fond farewells, we boarded our chariot and tried to settle down on para seats along the left side of the Herc. Footy gave me two yellow pills, which he said would knock me out all the way to Bahrain, but I decided to take them

144   Desert Cats: The RAF's Jaguar Force in the First Gulf War

after the Akrotiri refuelling stop, where I wanted to introduce Steve Farrow to the sergeants' mess following promotion.

After Akrotiri I took my pills. They worked! Someone shook me awake. 'Are we here already?' Of course, we weren't, the Herc had a radar problem and we were back in Akrotiri. But Baggers remained out of it throughout the wait.

27 November, 0300hrs. Bahrain and the usual routine: everyone running around like headless chickens, a quick briefing, and then to the hotel, our home for as long as it took. It was a grand establishment called the Diplomat. We'd been told there would be no more roulemonts, so we were it until the job was done. I reflected that this was not what we had been training for over the last six years. It was considerably warmer than the Arctic, and my accommodation was unusually palatial. And if things got serious, we stood a better chance of survival here than at Bardufoss. Lying on my king-size bed, I thought it best to accept the situation philosophically.

The handover from 6 Squadron was straightforward. It was good to catch up with Ian and Pete prior to their departure. I had a long chat with Vern Watkin, Warrant Officer 6, wished him well and took up the challenge.

On 4 November, I suffered my only bout of Bahrain tum, and went to the medics. They told me rest on my bed, drink lots of water and I would be OK in twenty-four hours. They were right.

During this period, we were inundated with gift parcels and cards, all of which had to be acknowledged. Some were particularly touching, especially those from the local

Looking over the city streets from the Diplomat Hotel. (*Courtesy M. Rainer*)

Squadron operations at Muharraq. (*Courtesy M. Cartwright*)

schools around Coltishall. One card arrived showing a picture of an attractive lady with very little on, asking if she could write to somebody. I handed it to one of my electricians and one thing led to another. To the best of my knowledge they are still married!

2 December was Scud Sunday. I was in ops with OC 6 Squadron for the morning briefing, listening to all the doom and gloom about Tornado serviceability. Our twelve aircraft were all fine, as always. The door opened and a Regiment guy poked his head in and informed us that the Iraqis had launched a Scud missile. All eyes turned to the front, but nothing was said. A few minutes later the same chap came in again and said another Scud had been launched. Eyes front again, response much the same as before. I looked across at OC 6 Squadron: 'Shouldn't we be doing something?' I asked.

From that moment, action. We returned to the flight line with instructions to arm and make ready. Vern Watkin and 6 offered their help but I thought, 'No, if we can't cope, we shouldn't be here.' All aircraft soon up and ready, armed to conform the then mission profile of low level. All the pilots were strapped in and waiting. OC 6 Squadron told me that the situation was not as serious as we first thought, but we were to go ahead, treating it as real. I told Craig all was well and gave him cheeky wink.

Boss arrived in the early hours. I met him for breakfast, gave him a full briefing as I saw it, and then we both enjoyed our omelettes and went our separate ways: him to bed, me to work. The first major change following Boss's arrival was dropping off the low-level missions in favour of medium level. The pilots cheered up immediately.

Scud Watch – ground crew on sentry duties, providing early earning against Scud attacks or inbound enemy aircraft. (*Courtesy M. Rainer*)

December continued much the same as November, with lots of flying and constant moving around until we arrived at three fixed operating sites: hangar (Chris Tracy), airport (Tony Tagg), and parade ground myself, each with four aircraft. It was a system which served us well.

Our Christmas carol concert was beamed back home. Beryl, my wife, says she saw me sitting on the wing. We ruffled a few feathers, but what the hell. On Christmas Day, Boss asked if the troops would mind if we flew. I said they would not, so all the pilots who wanted to fly and get this notable date in their logbooks did so. While I was in Engineering Control one of the lads came in to sign for flight servicing.

'What's the date, sir?'

'The 25th of December,' I replied.

'Thanks sir.'

I stopped doing what I was doing, grinned and carried on. That evening I had Christmas dinner with Tony Tagg and Paul Jerrard, my two stalwart flight sergeants. My daughter Jan had given me a Christmas cake when we left Coltishall, telling me to eat it at the correct time. The cake, which measured three inches by three, was divided up, followed by a Stilton and half a bottle of port supplied by Paul's wife, Ann.

On 31 December, 'N' burst all four tyres and had to be recovered, and of course Baggers got an AFC in the New Year Honours List.

*Above left, above right and below*: Jaguars under sun canopies at Muharraq with ground crew ready to assist with the aircraft. (*Courtesy M. Rainer*)

We were given a meagre pittance to feed ourselves, and Tony, Paul and I used to go out once a week and have a really good meal. One evening I suggested that we ask one of the pilots to join us. They agreed. We started with the Boss on 5 January. Next we took Craig and Shutty, they were joined at the hip, so there was no point trying to separate them, and it quickly became an accepted evening out. There were tense times for the officers waiting to be asked next.

Then, on 16 January, the war started. Here we go, I thought. I have never imagined it would come to this, but we had to get on with it. I was nearly fifty-four, with a year left to serve, and I realised that I was about to embark on something I'd remember for the rest of my life.

Our first mission went well, led by Strike with Stevie T, Roger and Mal completing the four-ship. I wished them all well with a handshake and a pat on the helmet, a gesture I tried to repeat on all the pilots' first missions.

The reality of what we were doing soon came home, with a Tornado lost on each of the first three nights, but we settled down very quickly to a routine: two shifts, twelve hours on, twelve hours off, a week of days and a week of nights. Weapon loads were known twenty-four hours in advance, so when the aircraft returned everything was ready to upload. Indeed, the guys got so adept it was alarming. Not the place for establishment turkeys. I recall getting a message that Hoppy had jettisoned his fuel tank; accordingly, a new one was prepared to await his arrival. When he stopped his aircraft, the lads had the new tank on before he had unstrapped and climbed out. He apologised for losing his tank.

'No, you haven't,' I said.

'I did, I felt it go,' he protested.

We kept up the ruse until he got into the flight office.

The sorties were always two four-ships in the morning followed by two four-ships plus two recce in the afternoon. Mostly bombs, but occasionally rockets. The lads were most concerned about their charges. When Shutty diverted, I remember the look on his mechanic's face when he did not return with the rest of the four-ship. When he did finally arrive, having refuelled at some godforsaken place, the young airman couldn't contain himself. 'Where the hell have you been?' he blurted out. Shutty proffered his regrets and promised it wouldn't happen again. I pointed out to the young lad that you don't normally talk to flight lieutenants like that. 'This ain't normal, sir', he glowered.

26 January, Australia Day, apparently, but more importantly, my birthday! I came in with Tony for the night shift to find the hangar decked out in bunting and 'Happy 54th Birthday Mick!' splashed all over the wall. There were good wishes from the detachment boss, Group Capt David Henderson, and the OC Eng, Wing Commander Greg Harker, followed by the cutting of an enormous cake. The lads gave me a personal

The Jaguar hangar, known as Chris Tracy. (*Courtesy M. Rainer*)

organiser, which I cherish and still use to this day. In one of our quieter moments, I was chatting with Greg Harker when he asked if I had done many overseas tours. I highlighted Germany as my first place called Wahn, now Cologne International Airport. He said he was there, and I twigged.

'Are you anything to do with Sergeant Lofty Harker?' I asked him.

'Oh yes,' he said, 'that was my father.'

He was surprised when I told him I used to babysit him back in 1955–56, but from that moment on we got on like a house on fire. Had Peter Driver and Martin Hepworth been there as well, it would have been heaven.

The night shift quickly became a week of rest. The day shift would do their utmost to rearm and clear all snags before we came in, which enabled 90 per cent of the night men to be back in the hotel by 1900hrs. Technically everyone blended in well. Whereas 6 Squadron had my personnel, we 41 finished up with technicians from all over, from Lossiemouth to Wildenrath, and the battle damage team from Abingdon. These chaps were excellent, carrying out in-theatre mods on two aircraft per evening and, more importantly, bringing 41's and 6's battle damage kits up to spec.

This became the pattern, with minor battle-damage repairs needed on only two aircraft. Our twelve Jaguars flew 618 operational sorties between 16 January and 28 February, and gave no trouble whatsoever through the whole conflict, and we did not replace one engine.

I spoke often with my OC Eng at Coltishall, Wing Commander Peter Dye, well into the conflict, asking if any of the Jaguars might need an engine replacement at any stage. So, with Tony and Paul I drew up a suggested programme based on hours, and on which aircraft were the biggest pain in the backside. Mike Rondot had also mentioned to me, quite rightly, that the windscreens on two aircraft were a bit ropey, but I was reluctant to change them in theatre.

I sent the info down the tubes to Peter, and a copy also found its way to HQ in Saudi. Soon afterwards we got a terse reply from some chair-bound engineering wonder stating that they would decide which aircraft were rotated, and when. The fact that we knew every inch of our charges didn't seem to come into it. The situation was resolved diplomatically by Peter's beautifully worded response.

The men found plenty to keep themselves busy, however, I drew the line at foul language painted on the bombs, but this didn't prevent them coming up with some excellent gallows humour about 41 Squadron landscape gardeners and the like. I got a message off myself, pointing out to Saddam how he had screwed up Christmas, New Year and possibly Easter. It was delivered by Footy at the second attempt. The nose art that appeared on the aircraft has all been recorded, and will no doubt be remembered much like that of the Second World War.

Towards the end of the conflict, I received a good luck card from Annie Fraser, our previous MO at Coltishall. She had been advised by her husband that 41 were out

Ground crew working on Jaguar aircraft. The second image is Jaguar XZ375 'Guardian Reader' with 1,000lb GP bombs fitted. The writing on the nearest bomb reads 'Chris Crusher'. (*Courtesy A. Emtage and M. Cartwright*)

there and wanted to send her good wishes. She'd spent a lot of time looking after us in the Arctic. It's lovely to think that she took the time out from her own labour to comment on ours. And hard to believe little Sophie is now thirteen years old.

On 10 March, a Sunday, I was asked by a WRAF movements officer when the squadron could be ready to move. I told her half of them could go right away, and so on Monday, 11 March, Paul's shift departed, followed by Tony's and mine on the Wednesday. We had a stopover in Akrotiri and then a direct flight home, and even had beer and wine on our VC10. There's a first for everything.

Unknown to us, a big reception was planned at Coltishall, with everyone there bar Ag and Fish. We had to be on chocks at Coltishall at 1400 precisely, which meant flying round the Orwell Bridge several times. Eventually we touched down and slowly evacuated the aircraft, to be met by the CAS, AOC and the Station Commander. I got handshakes and 'Well done, Mr C,' from the first two and an enormous bear hug from the Station Commander. He only let go when Beryl pointed out I was hers, not his. I was duly welcomed home by all my fellow WOs at Coltishall, and to cap a memorable return, Dickie arrived through the crowd with two glasses of champagne for Beryl and me, a fitting end to yet another 41 Squadron detachment.

One lasting memory for me is the way the lads all blended together from 41, 6, Coltishall and everywhere else. They worked hard and accepted their responsibilities willingly. Some were barely eighteen years old yet performed to the highest standards, only to be ignored when the plaudits were handed out.

Ground crew preparing to load a 1,000lb GP bomb onto the port wing of a Jaguar. (*Courtesy M. Cartwright*)

*Left*: A reflection of Jaguar XZ358 'Diplomatic Service' taken after heavy rain fall at Muharraq. (*Courtesy M. Cartwright*)

*Below*: Jaguar aircraft lined up at Muharraq, R–L: tail of XZ364 'Saddam', XZ356 'Mary Rose', XX962 'Fat Slags', XZ118 'Buster Gonad and his Unfeasibly Large Testicles', XZ119 'Katrina Jane', XX733 'Pink Spitfire', and XZ367 'White Rose'. (*Courtesy M. Cartwright*)

# Epilogue

Pilots and ground crew standing proudly together after the success they had achieved during the Gulf War. (Courtesy M. Rainier)

It would seem that, for this conflict, this is the last F540 entry to contain Jaguar Operations. The cease fire order has been met with the opposite, and yet still mixed, feelings that the outbreak of hostilities engendered. We are obviously relieved and pleased that it has come to a successful conclusion however, there is also a slight feeling of dread and disappointment at having to return to normal. Life will undoubtedly never be quite the same for those who took part. The engineers have continued to do an outstanding job and sorties lost due to aircraft unserviceability could be counted on one hand. In fact, the number of times the spare aircraft was taken would not require the use of any toes. With over 600 combat sorties flown this is undoubtedly an outstanding achievement. Similarly, the support personnel have worked tirelessly to ensure that the pilots received the best possible service. I would like to formally record my gratitude to all of the Jaguar detachment ground personnel for their hard work, their professionalism, their good humour and possibly most of all for their understanding. Lastly the pilots. They have been good and lucky. What more could we ask? On average each of the 22 pilots have flown 30 combat missions. To repeatedly fly into a combat zone uses a significant quantity of adrenalin and obviously imposes a great deal of stress. However, I am proud to say that each and every one of the squadron pilots withstood these pressures and day after day pressed home their attacks with deadly accuracy. I have been very fortunate to have been part of this squadron. It is the most cohesive, effective and professional unit I have ever served with. It has been a special experience.

W Pixton<br>
Wing Commander<br>
OC Jag Det

**11 March 1991**
Recorded from the last insert from the Operations Records F540 dated 27 February 1991.

*Left*: L–R: Flight Lieutenant Dick MacCormac, Flying Officer Nick Collins and Flight Lieutenant Pete Tholen standing by the nose of Jaguar XZ119 'Katrina Jane', celebrating the end of hostilities having safely returned to RAF Coltishall on 13 March 1991. (*Courtesy 41 Sqn, RAF*)

*Below*: L–R: Squadron Leader Chris Allam, Flight Lieutenants Pete Tholen, Mike Seares, Mark Hopkins and Dave Foote enjoying the end of hostilities in the officers' mess back at RAF Coltishall. (*Courtesy 41 Sqn, RAF*)

# Epilogue

13 March 1991, Jaguar's homecoming, lined up at dispersal having returned to RAF Coltishall, pilots being met by families and friends, Jaguar XX962 'Fat Slags' is nearest to the camera (*Courtesy RAFM*)

THE FINAL MISSION 15 MAR 91

LOCATION: THE BAR/COLTISHALL

MISSION: DRINK TILL YA DROP

TOT: 1700(L) – WELL LATE

LEADER REPORT: The hardest mission yet, with deadly resistance from wives/girlies. The team braved all this and pushed home many reattacks on the bar. Special mention of FLT LT Tholen who speed drank beyond the call of duty.

MISSION AOC'S REPORT: Nothing to add. I expect nothing less from the Jaguars.

*Appendix I*

# Jaguar Nose Art

Displaying nose art and designs on aircraft was historically a way to identify other friendly aircraft, however the practice evolved to express the individuality often constrained by the uniformity of the military. Regulations enforcing a strict no graffiti policy and the use of these sometimes-graphic designs still did not stop this type of 'artwork' being displayed during Op Granby from the Jaguar force and other aircraft types, from the Tornado to the Victor tanker. All nose art was primarily painted by two engineers of 6 Squadron, apart from Flt Lt Michael Rondot, who painted his own aircraft and Jaguar XZ367. Phrases and drawings were also depicted on bombs that were to be dropped. However, no offensive language was allowed to be written on the bombs, under strict guidance from Warrant Officer Mick Cartwright.

Mary Rose – SAC Dave Keely
Buster Gonad – Cpl Paul Robins
Pink Spitfire – Cpl Paul Robins
Debbie/White Rose – Squadron Leader Mike Rondot
Saddam – Cpl Paul Robins
Crusader/Fat Slags – Cpl Paul Robins, SAC Dave Keely
Katrina Jane – SAC Dave Keely
The Guardian Reader – Flt Lt Mike Rondot
Johnny Fartpants – Cpl Paul Robins
Rule Britannia – Cpl Paul Robins
Diplomatic Service – SAC Dave Keely

**Note:**
Pilots flew different aircraft and were not restricted to the dedicated Jaguar that had their name displayed on the side of the cockpit.

Jaguar XX748, coded U, did not display any artwork.

Ground crew stencilling a bomb tally to the fuselage of a Jaguar. (*Courtesy IWM*)

## Jaguar XZ356

'Mary Rose', coded N, piloted by Wing Commander Bill Pixton. He recalls, 'I went to see AVM Bill Wratten in Riyadh. I was given a postcard of an Arabic woman wearing

(*Courtesy W. Pixton*)

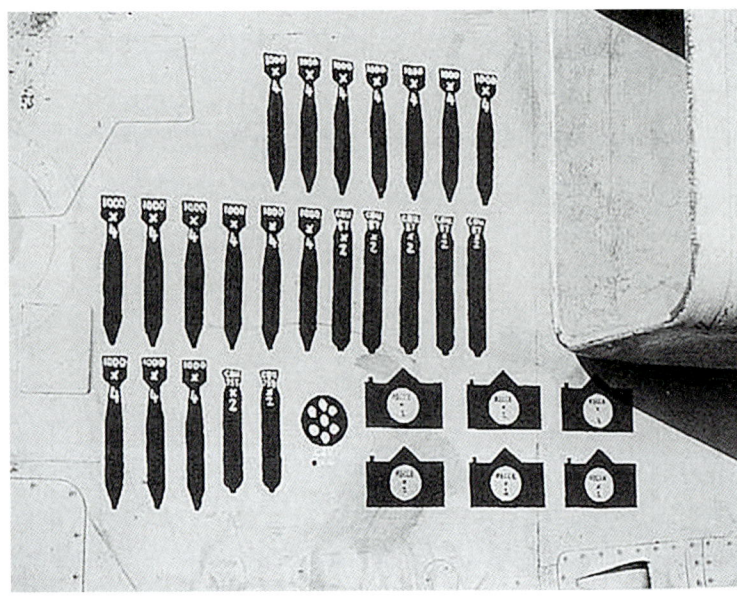

*(Courtesy W. Pixton)*

a burka that was blowing in the wind. Underneath she had stockings and suspenders on. People often mistake this for hair, but it is a burka. The name Mary Rose was my wife's name.'

## Jaguar XZ118
'Buster Gonad and his Unfeasibly Large Testicles', coded Y, piloted by Flight Lieutenants Stevie Thomas and Pete Tholen. It is another *Viz* character Stevie Thomas remembers

*(Courtesy S. Thomas)*

(*Courtesy S. Thomas*)

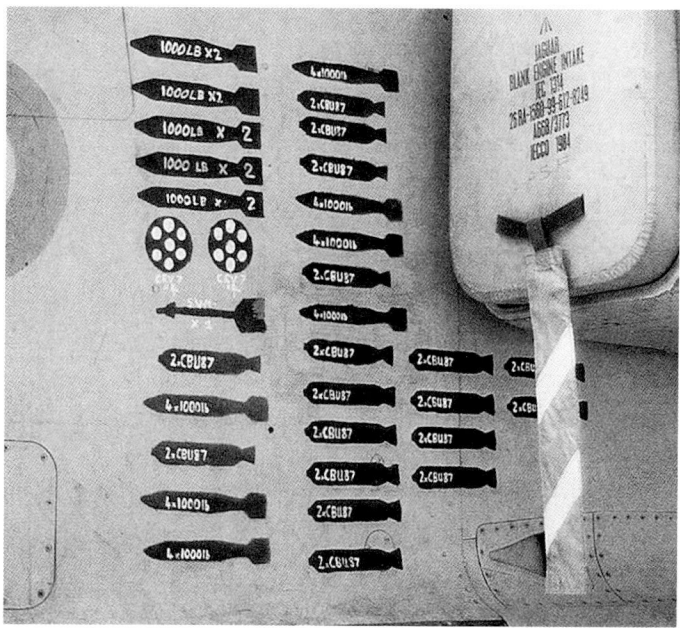

with humour, 'You had the forward line of own troops (FLOT) on the battlefield, and a suggestion was we should have had a forward line of gonads, which should never be crossed! Quite appropriate, perhaps when thinking of Buster's nose art.'

The FLOG LINE – Attention all squadron pilots:

> We now have new essential info to be annotated to all maps during the planning stage. Along with FLOT/FSCL/FEBA etc we now have the FLOG line – FORWARD LINE of OWN GONADS. It is suggested that this line runs parallel to, and no further than, 3 miles north of the Saudi/Kuwaiti border.
> 
> On reaching this line an alarm will sound a weak, whimpering sound. (Normally accompanied by major scrotum shrivelling.) On hearing the alarm, dispense with leader/wingman loyalty, stand your A/C on its ear + get the fuck out of there.

## Jaguar XX733
'Pink Spitfire', coded R, piloted by Squadron Leader Dave Bagshaw and Flight Lieutenant Pete Livesey. This unusual artwork design was related to Dave's past flying historic aircraft from the Fighter Collection housed at Duxford, including the Spitfire. With this, and the 'pink' colour scheme of the Jaguar aircraft, it was appropriately named. It was painted over a four-day period during the final week of the Gulf War and only thirty minutes from the official ceasefire. The artist Paul Robins had sketched out the design on scraps of paper earlier on the deployment.

*Above*: (*Courtesy D. Bagshaw*)

*Left*: (*Courtesy D. Bagshaw*)

## Jaguar XZ367

'Debbie', coded P, was named after the wife of one of the Jaguar's engineers, David Hall. It was later repainted and renamed the 'White Rose', piloted by Squadron Leader Mike Gordon and Flight Lieutenant Dave Foote, later Flying Officer Mal Rainier.

*Right*: (*Source unknown*)

*Below*: (*Courtesy M. Cartwright*)

An artist's impression of Jaguar XZ367 'White Rose' flying low over the desert. (*Source unknown*)

Squadron Leader Mike Gordon recalls why this nose art design was chosen and later changed. 'When the painting went onto the aircraft I wasn't bothered and would leave it up to the ground crew to decide. That is how I ended up with Debbie. One day when leading a four-ship with Mike Rondot, in the four he asked if he could change from echelon port to echelon starboard. When we got down I asked him why he had wanted to change, he said that he was offended by the quality of the artwork on my aircraft. I said that if he didn't like it could he repaint it and asked me what I would like. Being from Yorkshire, I said that a Yorkshire rose would be my first choice. Next day there was a Yorkshire rose on the aircraft.'

## Jaguar XZ364

'Saddam', coded Q, piloted by Squadron Leader Dick Midwinter and Flight Lieutenant Simon Young. This aircraft had the highest score of weapons released from any RAF aircraft, totalling ninety-six 1,000lb bombs, forty-one CBUs and eight CRV-7 rockets.

Squadron Leader Dick Midwinter recalls, 'I was trying to think of something to put on the nose and Douglas Bader had Hitler on his aircraft being kicked by a boot in the Second World War. I thought that it had an RAF and a Coltishall connection and all the right things to put on the design.' The artist started to sketch the design on the side of this aircraft at night, with only a torch to aid the drawing. The colours would be added in the day.

Jaguar Nose Art 163

*Above*: (*Courtesy D. Midwinter*)

*Right*: (*Source unknown*)

164  Desert Cats: The RAF's Jaguar Force in the First Gulf War

Group Captain Douglas Bader standing next to his aircraft with fellow members of 242 Squadron. Note the art on the nose of his aircraft is where the idea for the Saddam design originated. (*Courtesy RAF Archives*)

## Jaguar XX962
'Fat Slags', coded X, piloted by Flight Lieutenants Ted Stringer and Dave Foote. This aircraft displayed art on both sides of the nose. On the port side was painted

(*Courtesy D. Bagshaw*)

Jaguar Nose Art    165

an Arabian woman holding a crusader shield – she was painted with two left feet – nicknamed St Georgina. On the starboard side were displayed the characters Tracy and Sandra from *Viz* comic.

*Right*: (*Courtesy M. Cartwright*)

*Below left*: (*Courtesy M. Cartwright*)

*Below right*: (*Courtesy M. Cartwright*)

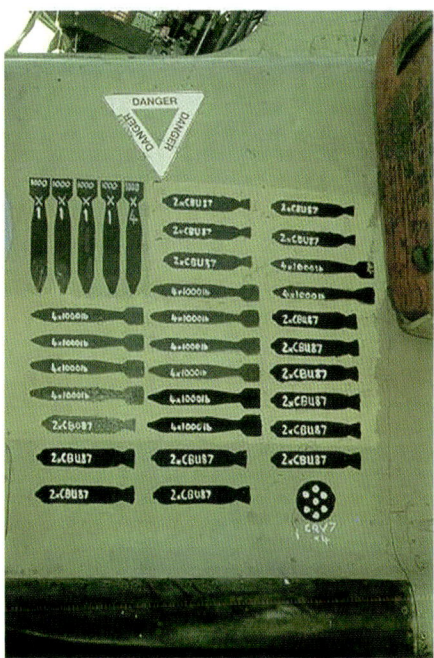

## Jaguar XZ119
'Katrina Jane', coded Z, piloted by Flight Lieutenants Dick MacCormac, Toby Craig and Flying Officer Mal Rainer.

*Above*: (*Courtesy M. Rainer*)

*Left*: (*Courtesy M. Cartwright*)

## Jaguar XZ375

'Guardian Reader', coded S, piloted by Squadron Leader Mike Rondot and Mike Seares. The author was informed that Squadron Leader Rondot had a friend who worked for *The Guardian*. Being sent a T-shirt from this friend, Squadron Leader Rondot was asked to have a photo taken wearing it and reading the newspaper. Instead of having a woman or similar cartoon displayed on the nose of his aircraft, he decided to have this design, which he drew and painted himself. However, this explanation cannot be verified.

(*Courtesy M. Cartwright*)

(*Courtesy M. Cartwright*)

(*Courtesy D. Bagshaw*)

## Jaguar XX725
'Johnny Fartpants', coded T, piloted by Flight Lieutenants Steve Shutt and Craig Hill. Johnny Fartpants was another character from the *Viz* adult comic.

## Jaguar XZ106
'Rule Britannia', coded O piloted by Squadron Leader Chris Allam. On the bomb tally artwork, a AIM-9L sidewinder missile is stencilled 'Truck'. This was from the combat

(*Courtesy C. Allam*)

sortie that was flown on the 17 January by Squadron Leader Mike Gordon when he fired a missile at a ground target.

## Jaguar XZ358
'Diplomatic Service', coded W, piloted by Flight Lieutenant Roger Crowder. This nose art was named after the hotel that the Jaguar force were accommodated in, the Diplomat. (Courtesy M. Rainer)

*Right*: (*Courtesy M. Rainer*)

*Below*: (*Courtesy M. Cartwright*)

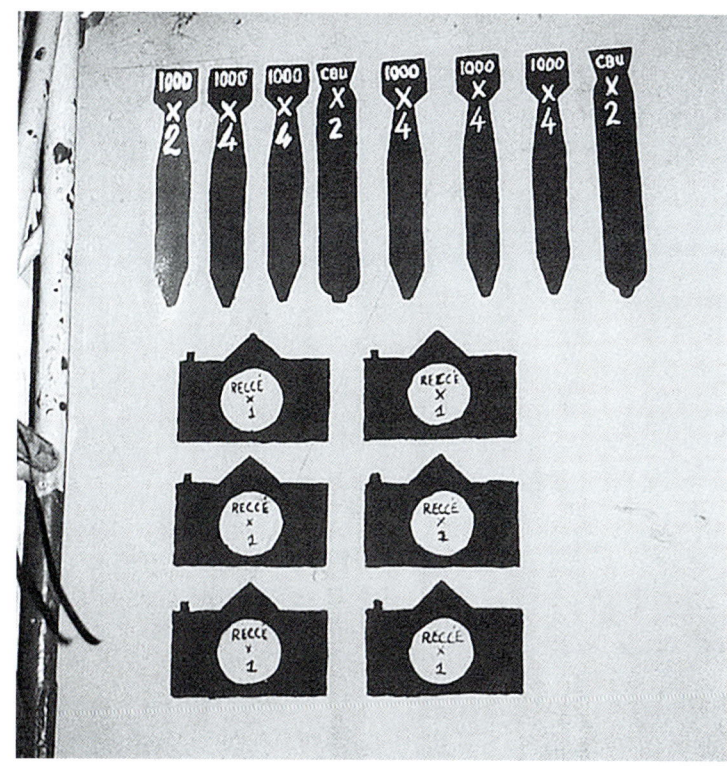

(*Courtesy M. Cartwright*)

## Jaguar XX748

Unnamed and coded U, piloted by Flight Lieutenants Mark Hopkins and Alex Emtage. An AIM-9L sidewinder missile stencilled on her bomb tally artwork reads 'Oops'. This refers to the mission flown by Flight Lieutenant Roger Crowder on 17 January when he accidently released a missile.

(*Courtesy M. Cartwright*)

Examples of messages that were written onto the housing of bombs that were to be dropped during the conflict by the Jaguar force, a tradition that went back to the First World War:

Warrant Officer Mick Cartwright standing next to a 1,000lb bomb with a message from both him and his wife, Beryl. This bomb was delivered by Flight Lieutenant Dave Foote on his second attempt on the target. (*Courtesy M. Cartwright*)

(*Courtesy M. Cartwright*)

(*Courtesy M. Cartwright*)

(*Courtesy Dazlyn Photography*)

(*Courtesy IWM*)

*Appendix II*

# Sorties Flown 17 January–27 February 1991

| Tail | Serial No./Name | Sorties |
|---|---|---|
| T | XZ356 Mary Rose | 47 |
| Y | XZ118 Buster Gonad | 38 |
| R | XX733 Pink Spitfire | 39 |
| P | XZ367 White Rose | 40 |
| Q | XZ364 Saddam | 47 |
| X | XX962 Fat Slags | 37 |
| Z | XZ119 Katrina Jane | 40 |
| S | XZ375 The Guardian Reader | 17 |
| T | XX725 Johnny Fartpants | 47 |
| O | XZ106 Rule Britannia | 35 |
| W | XZ358 Diplomatic Service | 14 |
| U | – | 36 |

*Appendix III*

# Aircraft Loadout

The following information is taken from an original document displaying the aircraft serviceability and weapon loadout for February 1991.

| A/C | US S | FUEL | SLOT | PORT | | | C/L | O/W | STBD | | | NAV | LIM RMKS |
| --- | --- | --- | --- | --- | --- | --- | --- | --- | --- | --- | --- | --- | --- |
| | | | | O | I | O/W | | | O/W | I | O | | |
| N XZ356 | S | T+ | 5 | ECM | 947 | M | T | M | M | 947 | PHI | AV | |
| O XZ106 | S | T+ | 8 | ECM | 947 | M | T | M | M | 947 | PHI | VG | |
| P XZ367 | S | T+ | 14 | ECM | 947 | M | T | M | M | 947 | PHI | AV | |
| Q XZ364 | S | T+ | 9 | ECM | 947 | M | T | M | M | 947 | PHI | G | |
| R XX733 | S | T+ | 6 | ECM | 952 | M | T | M | M | 952 | PHI | VG | |
| S XZ375 | S | T+ | 11 | ECM | 952 | M | T | M | M | 952 | PHI | G | |
| T XX725 | S | T+ | 17 | ECM | 947 | M | T | M | M | 947 | PHI | VG | |
| U XX748 | S | T+ | 10 | ECM | 952 | M | T | M | M | 952 | PHI | G | |
| W XZ358 | U/S | T+ | HGR | ECM | - | M | T | M | M | - | PHI | G | VIDEO |
| X XX962 | S | T+ | 7 | ECM | 947 | M | T | M | M | 947 | PHI | AV | NAV RUN |
| Y XZ118 | S | T+ | 16 | ECM | 952 | M | T | M | M | 952 | PHI | P | IMU CX |
| Z XZ119 | S | T+ | 15 | ECM | 947 | M | T | M | M | 947 | PHI | EX | |

**Key**

| | | | | | |
| --- | --- | --- | --- | --- | --- |
| S | = | Serviceable | U/S | = | Unserviceable |
| O | = | Outboard | I | = | Inboard |
| ECM | = | Electronic Counter Measures | 947/952 | = | Weapon fuses |
| C/L | = | Centre Line | T | = | Tank |
| HGR | = | Hangar | | | |
| T+ | = | Internal/External fuel | | | |
| O/W | = | Over Wing | | | |
| M | = | Missile | | | |
| PHI | = | Phimat Chaff dispenser | | | |

*Appendix IV*

# Mission Data

| Name | Hours Flown | Sorties |
|---|---|---|
| Wing Commander Pixton | 47 | 31 |
| Squadron Leader Allam | 40 | 31 |
| Squadron Leader Bagshaw | 32.15 | 23 |
| Squadron Leader Gordon | 41.55 | 31 |
| Squadron Leader Midwinter | 43.25 | 30 |
| Squadron Leader Rondot | 42.25 | 29 |
| Flight Lieutenant Crowder | 36.35 | 27 |
| Flight Lieutenant Emtage | 39.55 | 29 |
| Flight Lieutenant Foote | 36.55 | 28 |
| Flight Lieutenant Hill | 39.55 | 31 |
| Flight Lieutenant Hopkins | 40.05 | 29 |
| Flight Lieutenant Seares | 43.50 | 29 |
| Flight Lieutenant Shutt | 37.05 | 30 |
| Flight Lieutenant Stringer | 46.05 | 29 |
| Flight Lieutenant Tholen | 47.05 | 31 |
| Flight Lieutenant Thomas | 36.25 | 27 |
| Flight Lieutenant Young | 39.45 | 27 |
| Flight Lieutenant Craig | 41 | 28 |
| Flight Lieutenant MacCormac | 41.10 | 28 |
| Flight Lieutenant Livesey | 20.25 | 13 |
| Flying Officer Collins | 48.15 | 30 |
| Flying Officer Rainier | 36.05 | 27 |
| Total | 877.35 | 618 |

In Theatre of Operations:   3,921.50 hours
2,883 sorties
158 combat missions

*Appendix V*

# EMI Recce Pod

Squadron Leader Dave Bagshaw and Flight Lieutenant Pete Livesey standing beside Jaguar XX733 'Pink Spitfire'. These pilots were the 'dedicated' Jaguar recce pair. (*Courtesy P. Livesey*)

Data reproduced with kind permission from Spy flight data page.

Released into service for the Jaguar in 1972, the EMI recce pod was a large reconnaissance pod specifically designed for the Jaguar, operating in both low- and medium-level-type missions. It was initially designed from the legacy EMI pod fitted to the F-4 Phantom, and it was decided to utilise the original infrared linescan imaging equipment.

It was able to house a number of different camera suites, depending on the role that was to be flown. For low level, the pod was equipped with a Mark 7 camera with a

6in lens in the nose. And a fan of four horizon-to-horizon Vinten F95 Mark 10 cameras, two with 3in and two with 1½in lenses in the middle. The forward-looking camera and the two low oblique cameras were mounted in a front drum unit, with the two high oblique cameras mounted in a rear drum unit. Optically accurate glass windows were fitted across the drum skins at each camera position and, when not in use, these were shrouded by the pod structure. When required for use, the drums rotated 180 degrees, exposing the glass windows. The cameras in the rear drum were mounted on an easily removable role change module, forming part of the drum structure, and could be replaced by a similar module mounting a vertical F126 survey camera with a 6in lens, when the pod was required to undertake a medium-level role.

The EMI 401 infrared linescan imager was mounted in the rear of the pod and had an across-track field of view of 120 degrees. The unit could be offset 30 degrees port or starboard, giving a coverage between the 120 and 180 degrees sector.

The pod was also equipped with a self-contained air conditioning system and a DCU. The DCU was mounted in the pod structure immediately aft of the air conditioning unit, accepted inputs from the aircraft NAVWASS system and annotated the camera and IRLS films. The EMI reconnaissance pod was withdrawn from service in the 1990s and replaced with the Vinten Vicon 18 series 601 electro-optical reconnaissance system.

## Specification

Length: 5,800mm
Width: 648mm
Diameter: 635mm
Weight: 560kg
Magnification: 4 x
Max Range: 9.3km
Flight limit of 4½ G
Night capable

Flight Lieutenant, now Air Marshal, Edward Stringer, RAF, states the benefits of having photographic imagery that was taken from the LOROP camera:

> It was so much better to find a target with a photo than on a map; a map is just a picture of the desert. The desert is massively scared and marked. The Audi sign, it was four rings and it must have been a test track or something. It doesn't show on a map. The point being, desert was very easy to navigate around if you had photos. If you had a map you had a yellow piece of paper with some grid lines on it. If you are trying to find something next to a lake, wadi, or road, fair enough, but actually they are few and far between. Having a photo of the target was so much more useful.

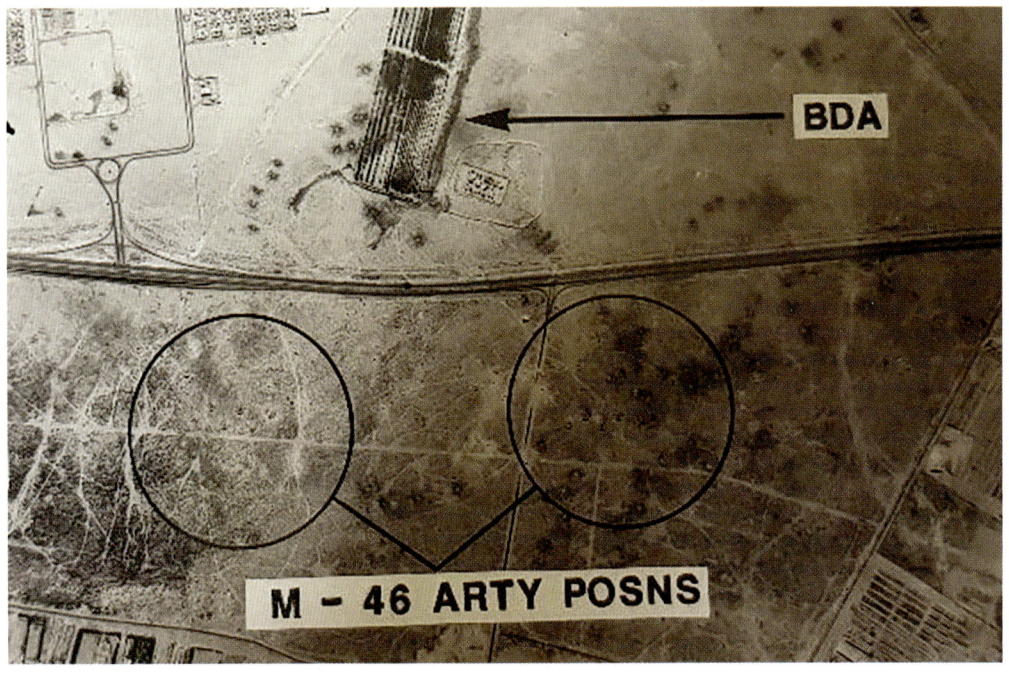

*Above and left*: Photos taken from the LOROP camera of Iraqi M46 artillery dug-in defensive positions and bomb damage assessment from a previous combat mission. (*Courtesy W. Pixton*)

A photograph by Flight Lieutenant Pete Livesey of Squadron Leader Dave Bagshaw flying Jaguar XZ356 'Mary Rose' in recce fit. (*Courtesy P. Livesey*)

A Jaguar fitted with an EMI recce pod. (*Source unknown*)

*Appendix VI*

# Gulf War Newspaper Article

The following extract is from an article that appeared in a number of newspapers at the time of the conflict:

One morning mission yesterday took them 15 miles inside Kuwait to attack SAM missiles silos. Squadron Leader Mike Gordon, from Dewsbury, West Yorkshire, said bad weather made it the most difficult so far. The one-man bombers took off from RAF base at Muharraq, Bahrain.

They dived out of thick clouds and pressed home the attack amid a storm of anti-aircraft fire. 'Flying in cloud, in formation over enemy territory isn't really what we like doing', said Sqn Ldr Gordon. 'I didn't notice any flak until we dived into the target area. There was cloud solid up to 15,000 feet. We came just about three or four miles short of the target and saw it down to the right.'

As they burst into clear air, Iraqi anti-aircraft artillery began firing. 'We pitched into a steep dive and then the orange bursts started, but at that time we were just concentrating on the target. Every time focuses. You look at the target and look at the release indications and to be honest the flak did not mean a lot to me. I released the weapon on the target, pulled off and that's when the chaff and flares were coming out quickly.'

When he saw the four 1000lb bombs striking the home he felt 'bloody brilliant, I can tell you'.

The air turned blue in the cockpit of Flight Lieutenant Steve Thomas, who was leading the pack of eight. He screamed in at 600mph after the 50 minute flight ... Only to find the trigger of his four 1000lb bombs was jammed. 'I have to confess to a few expletives in the cockpit', said Flight Lieutenant Thomas, from Wales. 'I thought I had the problem sorted out. It only became apparent as I was going into the target. I tried to correct it, but they didn't go off. That's the bottom line. It was a long way to go for it not to happen.'

Sqn Ldr Gordon flew in to protect his leader. He said, 'I could see Steve in front of me pulling off, and there was flak going off just at the back of his aircraft. I then started a jinking manoeuvre behind, and we jinked back into the cloud with flak going off behind us.'

All the other Jaguars forced their way through the anti-aircraft fire to drop their bombs. Flight Lieutenant Mike Seares, from Norwich, was on his first combat

A Jaguar silhouetted by the Arabian sun. (*Courtesy A. Emtage*)

Squadron Leader Chris Allam flying Jaguar XX725 'Johnny Fartpants' on a sortie on 31 January, his aircraft is armed with a 1000lb bomb payload. (*Courtesy C. Allam*)

182  Desert Cats: The RAF's Jaguar Force in the First Gulf War

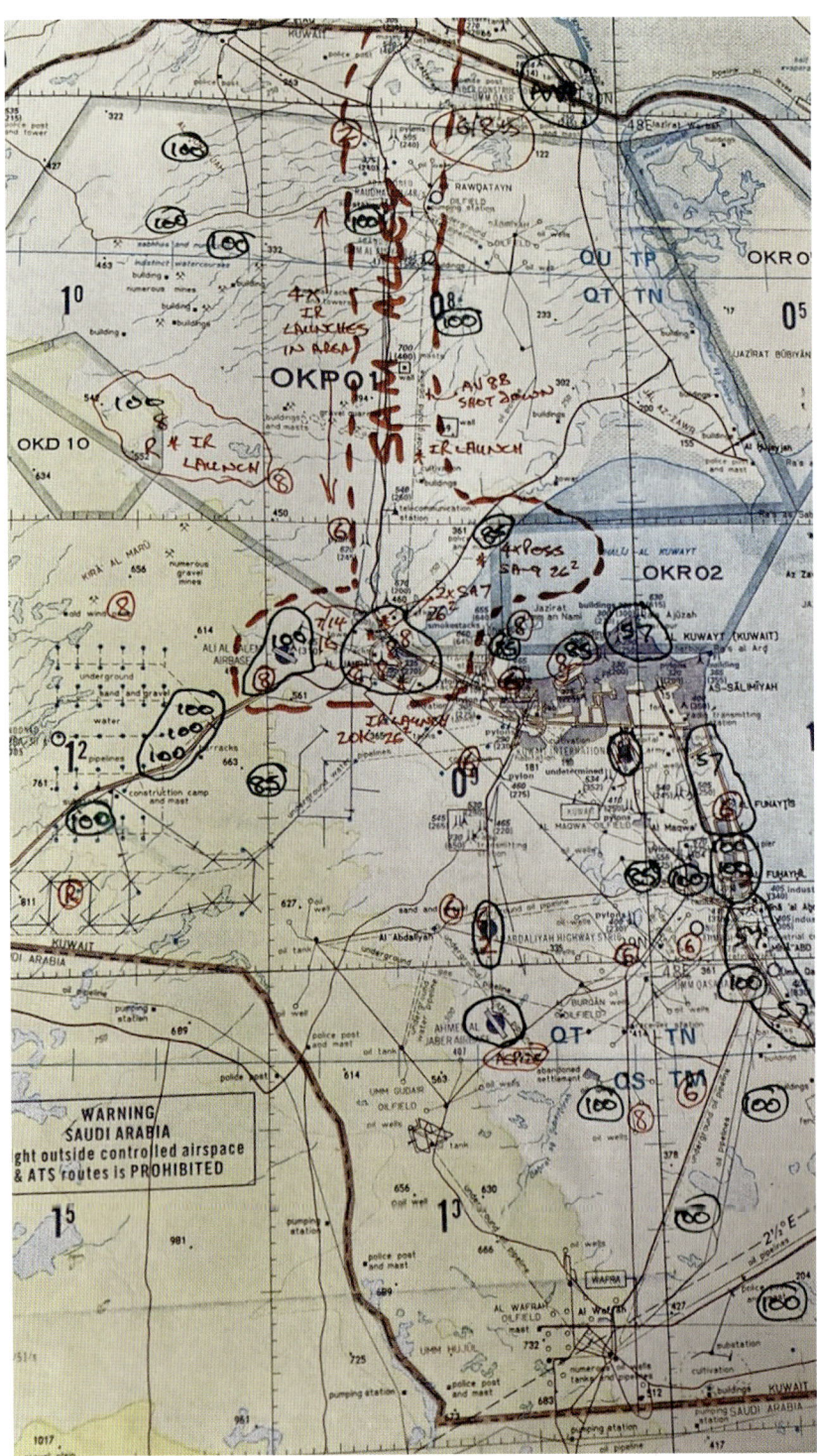

A operational flying map displaying SAM sites and other similar targets. (*Courtsey M. Rainer*)

mission. He said, 'I just felt relieved I was out of it. Just off the target there was a lot of flak. It was the longest minute of my life. I just wanted to get out. It was the first time I have seen tracer coming at me. Nothing can prepare you for it.'

Flight Lieutenant Alex Emtage, from Hampshire, said, 'When you see flak you think, "Hell's Bells, someone is out to get me." I only got scared after the bombs had gone and I got into cloud. You felt safe over Saudi air space but within a minute of the target you are concentrating on it. Having done what you had to do, you worry about getting home. The only thing is to get the hell out of there. I felt immense relief in getting back.'

Squadron Leader Mike Rondot, from Norwich, warned that things were going to get worse for the pilots. 'The days are getting longer, Saddam has still a lot to throw at us guys. We are just doing our job. It's the thing we are good at. We are a high-speed delivery service.'

The pilots' job is being made even more hazardous by the strict rule of attacking military sites only. They have been told to abandon the target if it cannot positively be identified.

Group Captain David Henderson, commander of the RAF base at Muharraq said, 'When there is AAA, anti-aircraft artillery coming up at you, it is a very, very disciplined and courageous man who holds on to his bombs to positively identify the target.'

The selective bombing rule gave one pilot a nightmare yesterday. 'He didn't identify the target and pulled off with a full load of bombs. You can't get up high enough and out of the flak as quick as if you had released your bombs. As he pulled up slowly from the target his number two slotted in behind him and dropped chaff as quickly as he could to try to confuse the enemy.'

*Appendix VII*

# Ground Liaison Officer

Major Pat King, an Army officer, was attached to the Jaguar roulemont at the time of the conflict. His primary role was to brief and communicate the coalition ground operations to the pilots before they flew on each combat mission, keeping them abreast with information hourly at the fast-moving pace of the ground offensive:

There I was in August 1990, fifty-three years old, sitting at RAF Coltishall as a Ground Liaison Officer with 41 Squadron, the Jaguar Recce Squadron. I had just mentally mapped out my last two years in uniform and was working on my pre-release courses and the like when Saddam Hussein invaded Kuwait.

The RAF put Coltishall on standby and then sent them off in a very short timeframe to Thumrait in Oman. The squadron sent was under opcon of 6 Squadron and was reinforced by pilots from 41 and 54 Squadrons. GLOs from 6 and 54 Squadrons departed.

I thought that I had missed out and sat back, watching and waiting. By November, with nothing happening, a roulemont was promulgated and I found myself with 41 Squadron in opcon heading for the Gulf, 6 Squadron having moved to Muharraq on Bahrain Island.

I had last been there with the Tigers [74 Squadron] in 1969–70 and found the place very changed. Roads and new buildings defied description, and they had reclaimed a lot of land from the sea by the causeway to Muharraq. The Bahrainis were delighted to see us back.

Due to the lack of accommodation, all of us on the squadron were housed in the Diplomat, a five-star Trust House Forte Hotel. Intensive training went on after our arrival. Christmas came and went with the TV carol service and with wonderful parcels from the Royal British Legion and numerous kind souls in Norfolk. We even got a proper Christmas tree donated by a shop in Coltishall village. By this time Saddam had started lobbing Scuds. We masked up and took cover quite frequently. Some hilarious scenes were witnessed with two legs down one trouser leg. One wag even worked out how to smoke a cigarette while masked up. Yes it is possible!

By mid-January things were looking ominous but I don't think that any of us thought that Saddam would see it through. Then we went to war stations four days before the ultimatum expired.

With three days to go we received our war brief. We were flabbergasted at the size of Operation Desert Storm. It had been planned by a genius. Fighters, air-to-air refuellers, fighter-bombers, bombers, Wild Weasels and other specialist aircraft had all been dovetailed together to make the largest raid plan ever seen.

D-Day approached. I was woken at D-Day plus 1 minute by the first Tornado eight-ship raid going to war. I leapt out of bed and saw them going out, no lights or beacons switched on.

I got into work at 0400hrs, just after they had landed. They were euphoric, no losses, and despite heavy AAA and SAMs, they had 'wellied' their target, and airfield. We then began Jaguar Ops, flying daylight raids only. We flew two waves daily for bombing missions and then added on recce missions after a couple of weeks.

Great excitement as the first mission left, followed by great tension as we waited for the Inflight report. Euphoria after both waves, no losses, and the last man in each wave had to be grabbed and reminded that he had not put in his mission report.

The euphoria quickly evaporated when it was learnt that the Boss and one of the other pilots in his wave had both suffered flak damage to their jets. We quickly got into a routine and worked flat out to produce all the information that the pilots needed. I was responsible for tasking the jets. This meant lots of calls to Air HQ at Riyadh.

In addition, I was responsible for ground intelligence and in making sure that all the mapping was up to date. I was helped by my clerk (Corporal RCT), a squadron leader Intelligence officer and an electronic warfare officer.

There were two complete teams as we gave twenty-four-hour cover to the squadron. I covered the days and GLO 54 Squadron flew out at the start of the war to cover nights. We were tasked against SAMs, log sites, ammo dumps, numerous artillery battalions and Silkworm anti-shipping missile sites.

In addition, we flew in support of Navy ops in the Gulf, and attacked shipping including a barge, fast patrol boats and a Polnocny tank-landing ship. The Jaguar Squadron was shot at daily right up until the end, and anyone who says that the air war was a doddle was not there.

Scuds flew our way throughout the war and after the initial worries over them we took them in our stride. Bahraini civilians carried on as normal, and the streets only cleared when the sirens sounded. All shop and hotel windows were taped. We were all so impressed with Patriot that we reckoned the inventor should receive a knighthood.

Integration between the various air forces was excellent and all of us worked extremely well together, whether Qatari, Bahraini, US, Canadian or French and so on. The skies were always very crowded and yet there were no mid-airs, and the plan always worked. The rule book took a back seat for the duration, yet everybody flew sensibly.

The resolve of the aircrew, whether Tornado, Jaguar, or others, was magnificent, and their professionalism had to be seen to be believed. The ground crews of both Tornados and Jaguars at Muharraq were magnificent throughout. Morale was always high and there was no lacking in confidence.

I never thought that I would go to war at my age, least at all with the Royal Air Force. Three of us had sons in 7 Armoured Brigade, which was an added worry for us. My son, Richard, was commanding an HQ in 21 Engineer Regiment.

It was unnerving to know roughly where he was and what he was doing during the land war, and I breathed a hearty sigh of relief when I learnt that he had come through safely.

I have come home greatly impressed by what I saw and by what took place, and I feel very privileged to have been a small part of it all.

Written in the squadron diary – *'Joking aside, Major Pat King worked long, hard hours, taking flak from HQ and pilots alike. All the while producing excellent results'.*

Major Pat King working at his desk, getting information prepared ready to brief the pilots before they fly. Written in the squadron diary, '0940, pick up the phone so double winged demi-god warriors of the skies think the GLO is busy!' (*Courtesy 41 Sqn, RAF*)

*Appendix VIII*

# Jaguar – Gulf War Twenty-Minute Presentation

After the Gulf War, Wing Commander Bill Pixton compiled a presentation on the combat missions and events that the Jaguar force conducted during the conflict. He toured various defence locations and gave a broad understanding of what was achieved and how and why command decisions were made.

The following are the notes from this presentation.

## Attention Getter

I am sure many of the pilots in the audience must have suffered, I as did, from numerous Hunter pilot stories that told of their exploits in the Middle East. They talked of wadi bashing, high angle rocketing with 3in drains, dive bombing and many other sand in the boots yarns. Some of you might even be those Hunter pilots! However, us more up to date pilots realise that there is little use for such outdated tactics and that low level is the only way to go! How I wish I had listened more closely to those crew-room Hunter stories.

## Introduction

I am Wing Commander Pixton, and I was the Boss of the Jaguar Squadron at Muharraq during Operation DESERT STORM. During the next 20 minutes or so I hope to give you a feel for the Jaguar Squadrons' contribution to the overall success of this operation. To achieve this, I'll show you where our geographical area of operations was and the threats that we faced within that area. Next, I'll outline the tactics and the weapons that we used to achieve our tasked aims and then I'll go on to cover the roles that we were employed in. Lastly, I'll run through the results that we achieved.

## Area of Operations and Threats

Our area of operations was dictated by our base location and our radius of action, which was similarly dictated by the amount of ordnance that we were required to carry. Single fuel tanks, 4 bomb fit with no tanker support gave us a medium/low/medium altitude radius of action of some 240nms. Two tanks, 2 bombs increased this range, without tanker support, to 310nms. Throughout the conflict we carried the -10 ECM pod on the port outer underwing pylon, the Phimat chaff pod on the starboard underwing pylon and 2 AIM-9s on the two over-wing pylons as well as flares in the ALE-40 dispensers. These self-defence stores were deemed essential and, apart from the AIM-9s, were used extensively on every mission. Our main area of interest therefore became the Kuwait Theatre of Operations (KTO), and we were tasked primarily against targets as far north as Kuwait City and as west to the tri-border area. As it transpired, our adoption of different attack tactics and the lack of tandem beam release clearance for one of our new weapons, meant our radius of action was actually greater than we had expected. This said, to have a comfortable combat fuel allowance proved to be a very sensible way to operate as there was a strange tendency to be rather heavy handed with the throttle during these missions.

Threats. The KTO had possibly the densest concentration of ground-based air defence systems within the overall DESERT STORM theatre of operations. This is a slide of our Int map at the end of the war, so it is a little less busy than it had been earlier. The green dots are AAA, and the red dots are radar-laid SAMs. As you can see, SAMs had become relatively rare by the ceasefire. The threat to aircraft operating at low level in daylight consisted of most of the modern Soviet-built IR SAMs, old- and new-generation Soviet radar-guided SAMs, modern Western SAMs such as Roland and the captured Kuwaiti I Hawk. Integrated into this air defence system was an amazing amount of anti-aircraft artillery, both optically laid and radar laid, and ranging from light 23mm and small arms fire to heavy calibre 100mm. Albeit we could under fly the threat envelope of some of the SAM systems and route around known fixed sites, the overall defensive capability of the Iraqi ground forces against low-flying aircraft caused a fair amount of concern in the crew room. Our other alternative was, of course, to attack from medium to high level. In this regime we could be outside the threat envelope of small arms fire, light AAA and most of his IR SAM systems.

Jaguar XZ106 'Rule Britannia'. (*Courtesy T. Craig*)

However, we would be in the heart of the envelope for a number of his radar-guided SAMs and still within range of the heavy AAA. On top of this, we expected, before the outbreak of hostilities, that the Iraqi air force would also present a significant threat, especially to medium- to high-flying aircraft. This of course turned out not to be the case; the only broadcast we heard from AWACS was 'picture clear'!

## Tactics & Weapons

Tactics. The major decision that we had to make was which tactics to employ, low level or high level. The argument in favour of employing low-level tactics included the following:

a. The aircraft itself and its weapons system have been optimised for low-level operations.
b. Our weapons stocks consisted predominantly of cluster and retard bombs, which could only be delivered from low level.
c. The pilots had been specifically trained over the years to operate in the low-level regime and this was where we initially thought we would be the most comfortable and indeed the most effective.

We were therefore leaning towards the opinion that you should fight the way you train and that we should stay low level. This was in fact the way that we planned and the way that we intended to execute our pre-planned 'D' Day targets should they have been tasked.

However, the arguments in favour of changing tactics completely and for us to go in high level were as follows:

a. Strange as it may seem, one of the major arguments supporting the high-level option was that the only squadron in the whole of the coalition air forces that was even contemplating going in low level in daylight was the RAF Jaguar squadron. This raised the question: What does everybody else know that we don't?

And it was probably this that made us look more seriously at the high-level option.

b. Probably the major benefit from employing high-level tactics was survivability. At least it would cut down the pure number of threats that we would have to face and certainly avoid any chance of a loss from a lucky small arms shot. Furthermore, if the Wild Weasels and EF-111s were as effective as they confidently predicted that they would be and if F-15 top cover was readily available, the threat from radar-laid SAMs and AAA and enemy fighters would also decrease substantially.

c. Another major advantage of attacking from high level was improved target acquisition. Large areas of the KTO are barren and featureless and, as we found during our training in Saudi, target acquisition at low level with few update points or lead-in features proved to be particularly difficult even in excellent weather. To miss a target in peacetime is bad enough but in war to fail to acquire the target is to risk all for nothing.

d. Other more tertiary advantages gained from going in high level were increased radius of action, easier target area deconfliction and better communications with allied ground units.

As the UN deadline approached the feeling that we would be more effective and that we would suffer fewer losses if we attacked from high level grew. This feeling was reinforced when we received the first 2 days FRAG and saw the massive SEAD campaign that had been planned. It was impossible to foresee the exact outcome of adopting either the high or the low option without trying them out first. However, the most sensible option to try first seemed to be high level, and that is what we did.

Weapons. The decision to adopt the high-level option generated a number of challenges for the pilots, the engineers and the staffs in theatre and at home. Our major concern was one of suitable and sufficient weapons. At the beginning of the

At low level over the Omani desert. This type of flying is where the Jaguar performed at its best. (*Courtesy M. Rainer*)

conflict the only weapons that we had available that could be delivered from high altitude were 1000lb freefall and laser-guided bombs and the recently arrived CRV-7 rockets. Furthermore, the only weapons in theatre that we had accurate ballistics for and therefore computed weapon aiming were BL755, 1000lb freefall and retard, and guns. Therefore, to ensure accurate weapon delivery we were effectively limited to freefall 1000lb. The problems highlighted by this were as follows.

a. We had a limited number of 960 MFBF and a limited number of freefall tails. In an attempt to alleviate the 960 fuse shortage, which became acute about 2–3 weeks into the war, we fitted single fuses to each 1000lb bomb, either 947 impact fuses or 952 VT, instead of the normal 960 nose fuse and a tail fuse back-up. During the last 2 weeks of the war we had run out of 947 and 952s and the remaining 960s were reserved for the LGB operations so we resorted to pistol and delay arming devices and dispensed with fuses altogether. We overcame the tail shortage by using the Battle Damage Repair team to modify retard tails for use in the freefall mode. The shortage of 1000lb bombs didn't quite become critical, mainly due to the purchase of significant numbers of the US-built cluster bombs.

b. The need for an area cluster weapon became clear very early on in the war from the targets that we were being given. The best weapon for the job which could be delivered from high level and which was readily available was the CBU-87. The time taken from identifying the need to the weapon being released to service and available in theatre for use was less than 2 weeks. I think that this achievement shows the excellent support that we received from the staffs in theatre and at home. Sadly, clearance to drop CBU-87 from tandem beams was never received and, similarly, the flight programme containing accurate CBU-87 computed weapon aiming arrived during the last week of the war. This said, the time from request to receipt of this flight programme, hot on the heels of another requested programme that I'll mention in a moment, was most impressive. In the meantime, we delivered CBU-87 in a computed aiming mode by using 540lb ballistics and adding a fudge factor into the computer for a specific set of release parameters.

c. The other weapon that we had available for use from a high-level, high-angle dive was the Canadian-built CRV-7 rocket. These weapons were initially bought to penetrate hardened targets, however they produced equally satisfactory results against ships, artillery and armour. The one and only major problem we encountered with employing this weapon was our lack of computed weapon aiming. With the vast experience of 12 practice rockets per pilot, it was not surprising that our initial results in war with an iron sight were a little disappointing. To achieve accurate release parameters, when avoiding

1,000lb GP bombs fitted to the starboard wing of a Jaguar. Note the AIM-9 Sidewinder fitted over the wing. (*Courtesy A. Emtage*)

# Jaguar – Gulf War Twenty-Minute Presentation 193

*Right*: A CBU-87 fitted to the starboard wing of a Jaguar. (*Courtesy A. Emtage*)

*Below*: High over the desert terrain, trailing behind a Tri-Star tanker taking fuel on board. (*Courtesy P. Tholen*)

Jaguar XZ119 'Katrina Jane'. (*Courtesy P. Tholen*)

weather and defences and when executing an unfamiliar attack profile with an unfamiliar weapon, to say the least, is not easy. I'm pleased to say that, again, the support staff came up trumps and a computed sight was available within 3 weeks of asking. This new flight programme combined with laser ranging provided the pilots with the proverbial death dot. Comments like 'you can't miss' became commonplace. In my view a weapon like this which provides a degree of standoff and significant hitting power should always form part of a ground attack aircraft's armoury. Towards the end of the conflict pilots were able to select and surgically destroy specific guns from a tasked artillery battery with this weapon. What a pity there were no steam locomotives in the desert! Although we had the capability, a workable profile and had suitable targets, we were never tasked with the Buccaneers on LGB operations.

## Roles

I'll now move on to the roles that we were employed in and these fall roughly into 3 categories, SUCAP/CSAR, Interdiction and Reconnaissance.

  a. SUCAP/CSAR. One of our more unusual tasks was SUCAP or CSAR, which stands for Surface Target Combat Air Patrol and Combat Search and Rescue. Both of these tasks were one of the same mission and flown primarily over

Gulf waters and in support of the allied naval force. These CAPs were flown throughout daylight hours as pairs of aircraft and made use of Victor tanker support. The only difference between the two types of sortie was the resulting target. For SUCAP our primary targets were Iraqi naval vessels, especially fast patrol boats that posed a threat to allied shipping. However, these missions were actually called in against a variety of enemy surface contacts including FPBs, light attack craft, barges and a Polnocny-class LSL. For Combat Search and Rescue the Jaguars were used to suppress enemy ground or surface fire in support of heliborne rescues of downed allied aircrew. Probably the best example of this was when the pair on CAP were vectored to Failaka Island to suppress AAA on the island that was hindering a nearby search for a US A-6 crew. These were missions that we had not trained for specifically and it took us a few sorties to get the weapon load right. Initially we used CRV-7 rockets, however, we suffered from the poor weapon aiming that I mentioned earlier. We then changed to BL-755 as the surface-to-air threat over Gulf waters seemed even at this early stage in the war to be relatively benign. This was a major mistake on my part driven in part by an abundance of these weapons and the availability of a computed weapon-aiming solution for the weapon. The one, and I might add only, mission to launch on SUCAP/CSAR armed with BL755 was, as luck would have it, called off CAP to help in the battle at Kahfji. In other words, overland in the Close Air Support role. The result of our only low-level overland attack resulted in one ZSU-23/4 and two SSVs destroyed. However, the volume of AAA, small arms fire and more importantly IR SAM launches forced one of the pair to jettison tanks, ECM pod and Phimat pod in a last-ditch manoeuvre to break missile lock of an in-flight IR missile. Fortunately, this was successful and therefore so was the mission. However, this experience confirmed our opinion that high level was the best tactic for this particular conflict. SUCAP/CSAR missions demanded a significant degree of flexibility from the pilots and little if anything could be pre-planned. We therefore decided that we must have accurate computed weapon aiming for the weapons used on these missions and that the weapon must be high-level capable. This limited us at this early stage of the war to the 1000lb plus guns as a back-up should the threat be low.

b. Interdiction. Our bread and butter mission became interdiction and accounted for some 87% of our total effort. Tasked targets included Silkworm sites, barracks, ammunition storage, electronics, SAM sites, armour and probably our most common target, artillery. Known, fixed targets were fairly straight forward to plan for and to attack. The tasked location was generally accurate and the imagery that we received from JARIC was adequate. Depending on the target, we used 1000lb bombs, either impact or airburst fused, CBU-87 and, once computed weapon aiming arrived, CRV-7. Initially we bombed in a 30-degree dive and aimed to release at 15,000, which gave us a minimum recovery height of about 11 to 12,000. However, as we gained experience, attacks became steeper and release heights increased. This produced two benefits. Firstly, weapon accuracy, especially with the CBU-87, improved markedly and, secondly, the minimum recovery height increased, which kept us above the popular AAA burst height of about 10 to 1500. To put some figures on the later attacks, we were tipping in from about 32,000 into a 35 to 60-degree dive and achieving releases at about 20,000. I suppose that we will have to file an IFR flight path to practise this one in the UK!

c. As the war progressed we moved away from fixed installations and concentrated more on mobile artillery. Self-propelled guns, towed artillery pieces and multi-barrel rocket launchers. This was where we started to have tasking problems. The Iraqis had prepared many more revetted positions in the desert than they had artillery pieces. In some areas the desert was literally covered with sand revetments. Our taskers had problems identifying active positions and resorted to tasking us against targets 'in the area of' a UTM. This forced us into an armed recce role, which was less than ideal although acceptable and possible from high level. These missions became known by the pilots as 'spooning around in Kuwait'! During week 2 of the war we received a new recce pod which I hoped might produce imagery which would put an end to spooning.

RECCE. This brings me to our final role, reconnaissance, which proved to be extremely important and attracted many converts from the pure attack pilots on the squadron. As with most of the systems on the Jaguar, the normal recce pod is optimized for low-level daylight operations, so we rather hoped we would not be tasked with recce missions. However, the arrival of the new Long Range Oblique Photographic Pod or LOROP changed this view. The first few sorties flown with this pod into the KTO were effectively trial runs and highlighted the limitations of the system. The 36-degree lens produced excellent and very detailed imagery from 25,000ft, however aiming such a narrow field of view camera at those heights proved to be very difficult. Similarly, the lack of man-made and natural features in the desert made it difficult for the PIs to accurately plot the position of any targets covered. Inertial data could not be included on the negatives as it is with our normal cameras. The solution that we came up with was to fly a recce pair on each tasked mission. One aircraft would carry the LOROP pod and the other would carry our normal pod fitted with the rarely used F-126 high-level survey camera. The 126 provided coverage at 1:50,000 scale as well as data matrix inertial position information. From this imagery the PIs could plot the position of targets covered by the LOROP. Until we had gained sufficient confidence in this method of operation we flew the recce pair against the targets that the Jaguar attackers were fragged with for the following day. The results were so good that the norm for attack missions was to plan IP to target runs on the 1:50,000 scale F-126 prints instead of the usual map and to select active DMPIs in the target area from the LOROP imagery. Pilots also carried the LOROP prints in the air for detailed target acquisition. JFHQ soon realised that we now had a workable recce system and tasked us in support of the British and USMC ground forces. Post-strike BDA and pre-strike recce of our own targets continued until ceasefire and undoubtedly improved our effectiveness against mobile targets. Indigenous recce assets might seem an expensive luxury, however, had we been forced to rely on other sources which usually boiled down to a FAX of a photocopy of a 3-day old overhead, we would certainly, at worst, have wasted scarce weapons on unoccupied sites or, at best, would have been unable to find active targets and have brought our weapons home.

## Results

This now brings me on to results. I suppose that the overall result speaks for itself; the Iraqis left Kuwait some 6 weeks after the beginning of the allied offensive. And although cast-iron BDA at squadron level was difficult to come by, the reports that I have had from people who have since been on the ground in the KTO would suggest that a lot of our targets were more heavily damaged than we might first have thought. Similarly, I like to think that the speed of the advance through the KTO and the small number of casualties incurred by the allied ground forces was due in some part to the effectiveness of the Jaguars. To give you some statistics, the Jaguar Squadron flew 617 sorties during the 6-week period and only 7 sorties were classified duty not carried out due to aircraft unserviceability. The breakdown by mission type is 72% interdiction, 15% SUCAP/CSAR and 13% recce. From a pure engineering point of view, we estimated that we could have comfortably generated about 28 sorties per day instead of the 18 that we were tasked with. However, the limiting factor proved to be the number of pilots in theatre. In my view, we had to work at our maximum sustainable rate because I did not know how long the conflict would last. To that end one mission per pilot per day was the most I felt that we could sustain long term. There was also a need to include in the programme some sort of regular stand-down for the pilots. The end result with 22 pilots was that at any one time 4 pilots were on 24 hours stand-down, which gave every pilot on average every fifth day off. This was agreed with AHQ and our tasking subsequently limited to 18 sorties per day. Some other interesting stats include: The youngest Jaguar pilot in the war was 23 and the oldest 54, the longest operational Jaguar mission, a SUCAP mission, lasted 5½ hours, we delivered 751 1000lb, 385 CBU-87, 608 CRV-7, 9,500 rounds of 30mm, 8 BL-755, 38 drop tanks, 1 ECM pod and 1 Phimat pod and we fortunately suffered light flak damage to only 3 aircraft.

## Conclusion

The unrefuelled range of the Jaguar dictated our area of operations and the threats in that area dictated our tactics: the decision to adopt high-level tactics despite the problems that this generated was in my view the best and most important decision that we made throughout this conflict. I still believe had we fought the way we had trained at low level that I would not have brought all 22 pilots home. However, even though we didn't use our low-level skill, the familiarity with high-workload situations that we had gained by operating at low level stood us in good stead for the increased pressures of war. By the time the ceasefire was called we had computed weapon aiming for CBU-87 and CRV-7 and the second buy of these weapons was en route. An R and R system for aircrew was about to begin, as was the roulemont of our stage 3 modified aircraft. In short we were ready and equipped should the conflict have continued. The only things that the pilots kept asking me for were bigger engines, twin fins and a bubble canopy. They also suggested that we should practise living in 5-star hotels in peacetime because you never know when you might have to do it for real. As a final statement from me, and you must remember that I am slightly biased, the Jaguar force deployed a 20-year-old aircraft in very short order, changed tactics completely and flew 618 successful combat sorties in the 6 weeks of fighting and, I'm very lucky to be able to say, without loss.

A cartoon mural of a 41 Squadron Jaguar displayed on a hangar door at RAF Coltishall. (*Courtesy Author*)

## Appendix IX

# Surviving Gulf War Jaguars

Jaguar XZ356 'Mary Rose', upgraded to GR3A. Disposed of in 2006. Private collection in Welshpool, Wales. (*Source unknown*)

*Right*: Jaguar XZ106 'Rule Britannia', upgraded to GR3A. Disposed of in 2005. On display at RAF Manston History Museum. (*Courtesy Flickr*)

*Below*: Jaguar XZ367 'White Rose', upgraded to GR3. Serving as an engineering training aircraft at RAF Cosford, DSAE. (*Courtesy RAF Cosford*)

Jaguar XZ364 'Saddam', upgraded to GR3A. Disposed of in 2005. Cockpit in private collection owned by Jet Art Aviation, Selby, South Yorkshire. (*Courtesy Jet Art*)

Jaguar XZ375 'Avid Guardian Reader', GR1A. Disposed of in 2002. Cockpit on display at the City of Norwich Aviation Museum, Norwich. (*Courtesy Flickr*)

Jaguar XX725 'Johnny Fartpants', upgraded to GR3A. Serving as an engineering training aircraft at RAF Cosford, DSAE. (*Courtesy RAF Cosford*)

Jaguar XX748, upgraded to GR3A. Serving as an engineering training aircraft at RAF Cosford, DSAE. (*Courtesy RAF Cosford*)

Jaguar XZ358 'Diplomatic Service', GR1A. Serving as an engineering training aircraft at RAF Cosford, DSAE. (*Courtesy RAF Cosford*)

Jaguar XX962 'Fat Slags', GR1B. The author is the custodian of the cockpit at RAF Coningsby. (*Author's collection*)

Surviving Gulf War Jaguars 203

Jaguar XZ119 'Katrina Jane', GR1A. Gifted in 2009 to the National Museum of Flight, East Fortune, Scotland. (*Courtesy Flickr*)

Jaguar XZ118 'Buster Gonad' GR3A, commissioned in 2010 by artist Fiona Banner at the Tate art museum, London. The complete fuselage of the aircraft has been stripped of its camouflage paint scheme, its bare metal polished. Once the display was finished with, the airframe was moved to Slimelight night club, London. (*Courtesy Thunder and Lightnings*)

*Appendix X*

# Recovery of Jaguar GR1B XX962 'Fat Slags'

On 2 July 2019, on a warm sunny day at Pembrey Sands Air Weapons Range, Carmarthenshire, South Wales, a group of like-minded people converged at the site for one purpose: to recover a piece of RAF combat history!

On 2 March 2009, the fuselage of Jaguar GR1B XX962 was struck off charge as scrap at nearby RAF St Athan in South Wales and transported to the Weapons Range at Pembrey Sands. It was followed by Jaguar GR1 XX966 on 12 May 2009.

These hulks were to be used as hard targets for aircraft to shoot live weapons at, placed on a trestle structure so the undercarriage would not sink into the soft beach surface at their new home.

It was not until late 2018 that the author was working at the range when he noticed the aircraft sitting on the northern side of the landscape looking very sorry for themselves, in a poor state with many parts having been stripped by souvenir hunters. One aircraft excited the author when he saw it was XX962, aka 'Fat Slags'. Having

XX966 and XX962 at RAF Pembrey Sands Air Weapons Range in 2012. (*Courtesy DIO*)

# Recovery of Jaguar GR1B XX962 'Fat Slags'  205

The cockpit section of XX962 being craned and transported from RAF Pembrey Sands. XX966 can be seen left wondering her fate. (*Author*)

completed thirty-seven combat operations during Gulf War 1, including the longest combat mission during the conflict, she needed saving!

With the help of many outside agencies success was achieved in recovering the cockpit section, which was removed and is now slowly being restored to museum display standard. Mounted on a trailer, it will be taken to events to show and educate visitors what the Jaguar Force did during the Gulf War and always remain part of RAF heritage.

Due to the aircraft being in poor state, it was decided that only the cockpit would be removed. This section displayed the nose art and bomb tally, and where the pilot, the human element of this historic aircraft, worked from.

*Appendix XI*

# Operational Awards

## Distinguished Flying Cross, DFC
**Wing Commander George William Pixton, AFC (8018671), Royal Air Force. Gazetted in supplement to** *The London Gazette*, **29 June 1991**

Wing Commander Pixton, the Officer Commanding No. 41 (Fighter) Squadron, operating Jaguar reconnaissance and fighter bomber aircraft deployed with his squadron on 9 December 1990 to the Operation Granby Royal Air Force Detachment at Al Muharraq, Bahrain. The aircraft are a key element of the United Kingdom's contribution to the multinational force formed in response to the Gulf crisis. The Jaguar Detachment commenced offensive operations against enemy targets in the Kuwait Theatre of Operations on 17 January 1991.

From the beginning of hostilities, Wing Commander Pixton had shown outstanding leadership and fortitude in leading and pressing home bold attacks against heavily defended targets. Using rockets, bombs and cluster munitions, these missions resulted in the destruction of a number of ammunition, fuel and other logistic storage areas essential to the enemy's war effort, and of long-range artillery and Silkworm missile sites that threatened allied land and naval forces.

Wing Commander Pixton's tenacity and presence of mind in the face of the enemy was characterised by an attack against a Soviet-produced Polnocny-class vessel. On this occasion, whilst on Combat Air Patrol in support of allied naval forces, he was tasked to engage and destroy the Iraqi vessel operating in the most northern waters of the Arabian Gulf. Undeterred by the possible danger from the vessel's machine guns, and showing great coolness and courage, he led a devastating rocket and strafing attack that left the vessel ablaze from bow to stern.

Wing Commander Pixton's quiet, self-assured manner in the face of great danger has been a magnificent example to all his pilots and his ground crew, and he has inspired his pilots to undertake bold, successful attacks against assets vital to the Iraqi occupation of Kuwait. These missions are especially notable in that they were undertaken by single seat aircraft operating at the extreme limit of their radius of action, with minimal self-protection and sometimes without allied air cover. Wing Commander Pixton's airmanship, leadership and exceptional fearlessness are in keeping with the highest traditions of the Royal Air Force.

## Squadron Leader Michael Andrew Gordon, MBE (2625943), Royal Air Force. Gazetted in supplement to *The London Gazette*, 29 June 1991

Squadron Leader Gordon, a Jaguar pilot and flight commander from No. 41(F) Squadron Royal Air Force Coltishall, joined the Operation Granby Royal Air Force Detachment at Muharraq, Bahrain on 14 November 1990. Jaguar aircraft are a key element of the United Kingdom's contribution to the multinational force formed in response to the Gulf crisis, and are tasked on air interdiction, combat search and rescue, anti-ship combat air patrol and tactical reconnaissance missions, both in Iraq and in the Kuwait Theatre of Operations.

Ever since the outbreak of hostilities on 17 January 1991, Squadron Leader Gordon has displayed qualities of leadership and coolness under fire that were a magnificent example to others. He was regularly met by heavy anti-aircraft artillery fire and surface to air missile defences on the approach to, or overhead his targets but, undeterred by the obvious danger and showing a complete disregard for his personal safety, he pressed home his attacks with devastating accuracy.

His exceptional fearlessness, skill, and his determination to meet the task laid on him inspired other pilots to press home their particular attacks, also with devastating results. Typically, on the 17th January 1991, whilst leading the first Jaguar mission of the conflict, Squadron Leader Gordon noticed antiaircraft artillery fire bursting close behind his wingman who, at that time, was concentrating on the final stages of his attack dive. With complete disregard for his personal safety, and showing outstanding fortitude and presence of mind, Squadron Leader Gordon flew his own aircraft between the incoming anti-aircraft fire and his vulnerable wingman to draw the anti-aircraft fire away from other aircraft. This selfless act undoubtedly saved a fellow pilot and a valuable aircraft from total loss and contributed to his wingman's successful attack. Squadron Leader Gordon's exceptional gallantry and quiet but dogged determination have been a shining example to all during a period of dangerous and demanding air operations that have undoubtedly saved the lives of many allied ground forces.

## Flying Officer Malcolm David Rainier (8029095), Royal Air Force. Gazetted in supplement to *The London Gazette*, 29 June 1991

Flying Officer Rainier, a pilot serving with No. 54 (Fighter) Squadron Royal Air Force Coltishall, joined the Operation Granby Royal Air Force Detachment at Muharraq, Bahrain on 11 October 1990. The Jaguar aircraft are a key element of the United Kingdom's contribution to the multi-national force formed in response to the Gulf crisis and throughout the air campaign they have been engaged in attacks against enemy positions in the Kuwait Theatre of Operations. At 23, he is the youngest single seat fighter pilot serving with the British Forces in the Gulf. Following the outbreak of hostilities, Flying Officer Rainier proved he was able to undertake operational missions that demanded flying skills and tactical awareness well above the level of competence that could be expected of someone with so little operational experience. Indeed, his professionalism, dedication and personal courage have been an example to older, more experienced pilots.

Throughout the campaign he worked tirelessly for the benefit of the squadron and nothing was too difficult for him to tackle. He demonstrated an unfailing enthusiasm for work and constantly strove to improve his knowledge and operational capacity. He quickly became a highly respected member of his formation and the work he put into pre-planning war sorties was a major factor in the success of many missions.

Indeed, on all of the 27 missions he flew during hostilities he showed great bravery and determination in fearlessly pressing home attacks despite heavy enemy anti-aircraft in fire and adverse weather conditions. Notably, on 19 January 1991, whilst taking part in a co-ordinated eight aircraft attack against two surface-to-air missile sites, his formation came under heavy anti-aircraft fire. Showing great presence of mind and undeterred by the obvious danger, Flying Officer Rainier promptly engaged this threat and scored a direct hit against the enemy position, eliminating the danger to the rest of the formation who were then able to safely attack their assigned targets.

Flying Officer Rainier has proved to be a most capable pilot whose bravery, leadership and airmanship are in the highest traditions of the Royal Air Force.

## Mentioned in Dispatches, MID
**Gazetted in supplement to *The London Gazette*, 29 June 1991**
Flight Lieutenant Craig Russell HILL (8028720), Royal Air Force.
Flight Lieutenant Peter John THOLEN (8027521), Royal Air Force.
Flight Lieutenant Stephen Richard THOMAS (8027264), Royal Air Force.

23rd January 1991

Dear Guest,

It is important that everyone is familiar with the hotel alarm systems and their meaning.

With effect from today the following sequences will apply:

FOUR INTERMITTENT RINGS OF APPROXIMATELY 10 SECONDS EACH FOLLOWED BY A SHORT PAUSE AND ANOTHER FOUR INTERMITTENT RINGS INDICATES THAT AN AIR RAID WARNING HAS BEEN SOUNDED IN BAHRAIN.

When this alarm sounds we strongly advise you to proceed to the ground floor and to follow the direction signs to the Grand Ambassador Suite which has been designated as a safe area.

PLEASE REMAIN IN THE GRAND AMBASSADOR SUITE UNTIL THE 'ALL CLEAR' SIGNAL HAS BEEN GIVEN BY RADIO AND TELEVISION.

Our standard fire/emergency alarm procedure will not change i.e. ONE SOUNDING OF THE FIRE BELLS (APPROX 20 SECONDS) WILL INDICATE THAT A DETECTOR HAS BEEN ACTIVATED IN THE BUILDING. THE ALARMS WILL THEN BE MUTED AND REACTIVATED IF A FIRE ETC. IS DISCOVERED IN THE BUILDING.

IF THE ALARMS SOUND CONTINUOUSLY PLEASE PROCEED <u>BY THE STAIRCASE</u> AS QUICKLY AND AS CALMLY AS POSSIBLE TO THE GROUND FLOOR AND EXIT THE BUILDING. PLEASE <u>DO NOT</u> USE THE ELEVATORS.

We would request that you please close the curtains before you leave your room. May we also suggest that when in your room you keep both Bahrain Television (Channel 5) and Bahrain Radio (Channel 4) switched on at a low volume.

Please do not hesitate to contact me or any member of my staff if you have any questions on the above.

Yours sincerely,

Brian Harries
General Manager

Information sheet located in every room of the Diplomat Hotel. (*Courtesy W. Pixton*)

*Appendix XII*

# Abbreviations

| | |
|---|---|
| AAA | Anti-aircraft artillery |
| AAM | Air-to-air missile |
| AAR | Air-to-air refuelling |
| AFB | Air Force Base |
| AFC | Air Force Cross |
| AGM | Air-guided missile |
| AI | Air interdiction |
| AIM | Air intercept missile |
| APC | Armoured Personnel Carrier |
| APU | Auxiliary power unit |
| ARTF | Alkaline removable temporary finish |
| ATO | Air tasking order |
| AVM | Air Vice Marshal |
| AWAC | Airborne early warning and control |
| BDA | Bomb damage assessment |
| BFPO | British Forces Post Office |
| BGM | Ballistic guided missile |
| CALCM | Conventional air-launched cruise missile |
| CAP | Counter air patrol |
| CAS | Close air support |
| CBU | Cluster bomb unitary |
| CCIP | Continuously computed impact point |
| CMDS | Countermeasure dispenser system |
| CRV | Canadian rocket vehicle |
| CSAR | Combat search and rescue |
| CTTO | Central Trials and Tactics Organisation |
| CVBG | Carrier Battle Group |
| DCU | Data converter unit |
| DFC | Distinguished Flying Cross |
| DH | Direct hit |
| DMPI | Desired mean point impact |
| E&E | Escape and evasion |
| ECM | Electronic countermeasure |

| | |
|---|---|
| EWO | Electronic warfare officer |
| FAC | Forward air controller |
| FAC(A) | Forward air controller airborne |
| GCAS | Ground close air support |
| GEC | General Electric Company |
| GLO | Ground liaison officer |
| GP | General purpose |
| GR | Ground reconnaissance |
| HARM | High-speed anti-radiation missile |
| HE | High explosive |
| HMS | Her Majesty's Ship |
| HUD | Head-up display |
| HVAR | High Velocity Aircraft Rocket |
| IFF | Identification friend or foe |
| IMC | Instrument Metrological Conditions |
| IRLS | Infrared linescan |
| IP | Initial point |
| INS | Inertial navigation system |
| JFHQ | Joint Forces Headquarters |
| JTAC | Joint terminal attack controller |
| KTO | Kuwait Theatre Operations |
| LFA | Low-flying area |
| LOROP | Vinten/Long-range oblique photography |
| LRMTS | Laser ranger and marked seeker |
| MFBF | Multi-Function Bomb Fuse |
| MID | Mentioned in Dispatches |
| MoD | Ministry of Defence |
| MRL | Multiple rocket launcher |
| MSD | Mean sea level |
| NAVWASS | Navigation and weapon-aiming sub system |
| NBC | Nuclear biological chemical |
| OC | Officer commanding |
| OCU | Operational conversion unit |
| OLF | Operational low flying |
| PMD | Projected map display |
| QFI | Qualified flying instructor |
| QWI | Qualified weapons instructor |
| RAF | Royal Air Force |
| RAM | Radar-absorbent material |
| RSAF | Royal Saudi Air Force |

| | |
|---|---|
| RTB | Return to base |
| RWR | Radar warning receiver |
| SAM | Surface-to-air missile |
| SA | Surface-to-air |
| SEAD | Suppression enemy air defence |
| SOAF | Sultan of Oman Armed Forces |
| SSV | Soft-skinned vehicle/Strategic sealift vessel |
| STANEVAL | Standards & evaluation |
| SUCAP | Surface combat air patrol |
| SWARM | Surface wave radar-absorbent material |
| TACAN | Tactical air navigation system |
| TFS | Tactical Fighter Squadron |
| TOT | Time on target |
| UHF | Ultra high frequency |
| USAF | United States Air Force |
| USMC | United States Marine Corps |
| USS | United States Ship |
| VHF | Very high frequency |
| XCAS | X close air support |
| XO | Executive officer |

# Index

1000lb G.P. [weapon], 12, 14, 16, 22, 25–30, 32, 36, 39, 109, 180, 191, 195, 197
2S1 [arty], 22, 35
226 OCU, 128
6 Squadron, 58, 90–1, 142, 149, 151, 184
41 Squadron, 67, 71, 90–1, 102, 111, 142, 149, 151, 184, 207
54 Squadron, 7, 128, 139, 142–3, 184–5, 208
74 Squadron, 184

A-6 [aircraft], 18, 26, 52, 98, 195
A-10 [aircraft], 93, 95, 120
Aden, cannon, 7, 81, 85, 94, 104, 197
AFC [award], 90, 146, 207
AH-64 [aircraft], 1
AIM-9 [missile], 5, 7, 17, 74, 80–1, 124, 127, 168, 170, 187–88, see Sidewinder
Akrotiri, RAF [airbase], 87, 144, 151
Al-Ahsa [airbase], 102
Al-Muharraq [airbase], 15, 24–5, 71, 79, 83, 87, 94, 102, 104, 109, 130, 180, 183–4, 186–7, 207–8
Allam, Chris, 46–50, 84, 91, 168
*America*, USS [ship], 2
Armee de l' Air, 102
AWACs [aircraft], 17, 22–3, 49, 62, 81, 93, 110, 189

B-52 [aircraft], 2–3
Bader, Gp Cpt Douglas, 162

Bagshaw, David, 42, 51–8, 85, 159
Bahrain, 23, 25, 46–7, 50–1, 60, 67, 74, 79, 84, 87–8, 91, 99–100, 102, 109–10, 112, 118–19, 128, 134–6, 143–4, 180, 184–5, 207–208
Barratt, Tom, 142
BBC, 123
BL-775, [weapon], 9, 23, 67, 89, 136, 191, 195
Brawdy, RAF [airbase], 118
*Brazen*, HMS [ship], 24
Brize Norton, RAF [airbase], 46, 67, 84
Buccaneer [aircraft], 7, 42, 79, 194

C-130 [aircraft], 46, 51, 67, 84, 87, 91, 135–6, 142–4
Cairo, 107
Canberra [aircraft], 116
Cartwright, Mick, 51, 104, 114, 119, 142, 156
CBU-87 [weapon], 3, 8–9, 71, 119, 124, 136, 189, 191, 195–8, 207
Collins, Nick, *XIII*, 46, 91–3, 102, 113, 120
Collister, Nick, 67
Coltishall, RAF [airbase], 5, 24, 51, 60, 90–2, 107, 118, 128, 142, 145–6, 149, 151, 162, 184, 208
Connolly, Jerry, 90–1, 102
Connor, Nick, 102
CNN, 47, 51, 92

Craig, Toby, 8–9, 58–66, 71, 92, 135, 145, 147, 166
Crowder, Roger, 46, 74, 92, 104, 107, 147, 169–70
CRV-7 [weapon], 8, 12, 15, 18, 22–3, 25, 39, 40, 69, 71, 89, 112, 120, 124–5, 130, 162, 191, 195–8

DFC [award], 79, 100, 109, 207–208
Dhahran, 15, 58, 112
Duxford, RAF [airbase], 159
Dye, Peter, 149

EF-111 [aircraft], 1–2, 189
Elliot, Alex, 71
Emtage, Alex, 67–74, 79, 118, 170, 183

F-4(G) [aircraft], 2, 58, 176, 185, 189, *see* Wild Weasel
F-15E [aircraft], 1, 17, 189
F-117A [aircraft], 2
Failaka [island], 107, 195
Farrow, Steve, 144
Foote, David, 47–9, 51, 102, 143, 149, 161, 164

GLO [role], 6, 47–8, 50, 109, 184–6
Gordon, Mike, 6, 74–9, 91–2, 113, 118–19, 161–2, 180, 208
Granby, 1, 4–5, 156, 207–208

Hall, David, 161
Harker, Gregg, 148–9
Henderson, Gp Cpt David, 148, 183
Hewlett, Tim, 135
HF [radio], 6
Hill, Craig, 46–8, 147, 168, 209
Hine, Sir Patrick, ACM, 42
Hitler, Adolf, 162

Hollett, Trev, 142
Hopkins, Mark, 7, 67, 69, 79–83, 134, 148, 170

Jerrard, Paul, 146
*John F. Kennedy* USS [ship], 2

Khafji, 107
King, Pat, 109, 184–6
Kuwait, 1–3, 12, 21, 25, 29, 32, 35–9, 46, 49, 54, 60–62, 68, 77, 79, 92, 95, 98, 102, 104, 109–10, 112, 130, 136, 138, 159, 180, 184, 188, 196–7, 207–208

Last, Rob, 102
Lean, Pete, 142
Livesey, Pete, 52, 54, 84–7, 91–2, 159
*London*, HMS, 23
LOROP [camera], 21–2, 25–6, 32–3, 35–6, 40, 52, 54, 85, 177, 196–7
Lossiemouth, RAF [airfield], 128, 149
Lyneham, RAF [airfield], 142

MacCormac, Dick, 8, 58, 60, 64, 92, 135–6, 166
MBE [award], IX, 208
McFadyen, AM Ian, 42
McGregor, Gp Cpt Doug, 118
MID [award], 209
*Midway*, USS [ship], 2
Midwinter, Dick, 87–90, 92, 136–7, 162
Mig [aircraft], 52
Mirage [aircraft], 2, 17, 21, 107, 124
*Missouri*, USS [ship], 98, 136
MOD, 4
M46 [arty], 8, 17–18, 35, 60
MH-53 [aircraft], 1

Neilson, Bob, 84
Nelson, Ian, 142

Oman, 4–5, 7, 51, 58, 90, 114, 130, 139, 184

Pembrey Sands, VI, 204
Pixton, Bill, 46, 78, 80, 92–102, 116–120, 122, 142, 157, 187, 209
Polnocny [ship], 98–9, 122, 185, 195, 207

QFI [role], 128
QWI [role], 60, 78, 91, 109, 111–12, 122, 128–30

Rainer, Mal, 58, 91–3, 102–109, 147, 161, 166, 208
*Ranger*, USS [ship], 2
Republican Guard, 39–40, 81, 93
Reynolds, Darren, 142
Riyadh, 1, 48, 52, 84, 92, 135, 157, 185
Rondot, Mike, 78, 81, 91, 110, 149, 156, 162, 167, 183
RSAF, 39

SA-2 [missile], 14–15, 29, 32–3, 39–40, 69, 79, 81, 87, 109, 134
SA-6 [missile], 37, 39–41, 60
SA-8 [missile], 39, 40–41, 60, 122, 129-130
SA-9 [missile], 87
Saddam Hussein, 2, 46-7, 54, 104, 149, 183, 184
*Saratoga*, USS [ship], 2
Saudi Arabia, 1–3, 23, 38, 46, 51, 58, 79, 94, 110, 113, 128, 149, 159, 183, 190
Seares, Mike, 8, 109–10, 167, 180
Shutt, Steve, 46–7, 102, 147–8, 168
Silkworm [missile], 8, 18, 20–2, 25–7, 30–1, 61, 77, 138, 185, 195, 207
SOAF, 7
St Athan, RAF [airbase], 204
STANEVAL, 128
Stringer, Ted, 92–3, 111–17, 120, 164, 177

Tagg, Tony, 146
*Theodore Roosevelt*, USS [ship], 2
Tholen, Pete, 60, 91–3, 98, 107, 112, 118–28, 158, 158, 209
Thomas, Stevie, 52, 60, 71, 74–5, 79, 91, 104, 109–112, 120, 128–35, 147, 158
Thumrait [airfield], 4, 58, 184
Tornado [aircraft], VIII, 3, 8, 42, 46–7, 50, 79, 81, 84, 88, 92, 104–105, 109, 116, 122, 125, 135, 145, 148, 156, 185–6

Upavon, RAF [airbase], 118
USAF, 1–2, 16, 52, 58, 62, 112, 120, 123
US Army, 1
USMC, 18, 26, 36–7, 39–40, 42, 58, 62, 197
USN, 3, 62, 77, 98
Uxbridge, RAF [airbase], 142

VC10 [aircraft], 58, 90, 107, 151
VHF, 6

Watkin, Vern, 144–5
Wilson, Andrew, 1
Wratten, AVM William, 1, 50, 157

XX748, 77, 88, 120, 156, 170
XX752, Johnny Fartpants, 79, 92, 104
XX962, Fat Slags, 54, 114, 164, 204–206
XX966, 204
XZ106, Rule Britannia, 52, 69, 74, 81, 112, 168
XZ118, Buster Gonad, 48, 113, 158-159
XZ119, Katrina Jane, 128, 136, 166
XZ356, Mary Rose, 85, 122, 136, 157–8
XZ358, Diplomatic Service, 60, 169
XZ364, Saddam, 87, 98, 122, 162–4
XZ367, White Rose, 113, 156, 161–2

Young, Simon, 88–9, 92, 135–41, 162

ZSU-234 [weapon], 23, 28, 89, 137, 195